THE

WARREN SPAHN

STORY

By *MILTON J. SHAPIRO*

JULIAN MESSNER, INC. • NEW YORK

Published by Julian Messner, Inc.
8 West 40 Street, New York 18

Published simultaneously in Canada
by The Copp Clark Publishing Co. Limited

Printed in the United States of America
Library of Congress Catalog Card No. 58-7258

Photographs used with the permission of Wide World Photos

To my brother Al, who bought my first baseball glove, but left in the middle of the game

With grateful acknowledgment to Bill Carr
for his help in the preparation of this book

The Warren Spahn Story

Chapter One ·

Staff Sergeant Warren E. Spahn glanced anxiously up at the sky as the opening bursts of fire belched from the antiaircraft guns dug in around Remagen Bridge. "Stukas again," he muttered bitterly to himself. The ugly black specks of the Nazi dive bombers circled lazily, like buzzards, high over the bridge, then peeled off and angled for the attack, diving steeply through the dirty brown puffs of ack-ack.

Spahn, standing at the western end of the bridge, watched the Stukas in their dive for a brief moment, then ran in a half crouch toward the center of the structure, where his platoon of engineers was working desperately to repair the vital span across the Rhine. The first bombs struck wide of their mark, landing in the river and sending geysers of spray high into the air. The bridge rocked and swayed from the impact of the near misses and the vibration of the thundering ack-ack guns.

The engineers continued their work calmly throughout the bombardment, Sergeant Spahn going from man to man, urging them on, though he knew they needed little reminding of the task in front of them. The Battle of the

Bulge, three months before, had welded the green engineers into tough fighting men; they were a team now, and the daily attacks by German planes and artillery barely made them pause in their work.

Spahn had worked his back toward the end of the bridge when his battle-trained reflexes made him turn his head at the sound of a roaring airplane engine. A Stuka had evaded the deadly concentration of defensive fire and was swooping in for a strafing run at the men on the bridge.

"Down!" Spahn yelled to his men, and threw himself flat on the ground. The engineers dropped in their tracks. All they could do then was hug the deck of the bridge on their bellies and pray, as the Stuka's machine gun slugs tore into the wooden planking, banged and ricocheted off steel girders and equipment. A GI screamed as he was hit. Then another. Finally the Stuka was past them and over the town. Medics ran up and began patching the wounded men. The engineers rose slowly to their feet and went back to work.

The attack was over. Sergeant Spahn checked the two wounded men to see if they were from his platoon; they weren't, and he returned to the center of the bridge to continue supervision of the repairs.

"I want a squad to clean up the mess those planes just made," he told a young corporal. "Get any badly damaged equipment off to one side, make up a list and let's get it replaced. Any timber that's chewed up dump over the side. On the double."

"Right, Sarge."

Sergeant Spahn walked over to where his welders were working on the steel supports for the bridge deck. "You guys got enough gas for those torches?"

"We're okay, Sarge."

Spahn nodded and walked on. He leaped into the cab of a crane that was tightening cables. "How are we doing on that truss?" he asked the operator.

"Tough job, Sarge," the GI replied. "The Krauts set off their biggest demolition charge right under here, but we're doing our best."

"Okay. Let's keep after it. There's another convoy due through here in a couple of hours. The Old Man's plenty worried about this bridge holding up."

His platoon checked out, Sergeant Spahn strode to the end of the bridge where Captain Francis Goodwin, the engineer combat supply officer, was talking with Lieutenant Colonel Clayton A. Rust, commanding officer of Spahn's outfit—the 276th Engineer Combat Battalion.

Spahn snapped a salute at the two officers, who had remained in the open all during the Stuka attack, then continued on into the town of Remagen to check with his company commander on his orders for the day. For seven straight days, since the morning of March 10, 1945, when the 276th had moved into Remagen, the routine had remained unchanged: "Bridge repair will continue in shifts around the clock."

And continue it did, without halt, through air attacks, continual artillery bombardment and daily plastering by one of the Nazis' giant V-2 bombs.

Spahn's company commander was quartered in a

house at the eastern end of Remagen, not far from the bridge itself. Spahn pushed open the door and saluted.

"Sit down, Sergeant." The officer lit a cigarette. "How much more time you think we'll need on this job?"

Spahn calculated. "Another twenty-four hours, maybe. The big trouble is that truss at the south side of the bridge, about two thirds of the way across. The heavy demolition went off there. We've got a crane working on the cables, but it's been a tough haul."

The officer blew a cloud of smoke at the ceiling and sighed wearily. "I know. And that shelling we've been getting every day hasn't helped any. Any casualties this morning?"

"No, sir. Two men were clipped by the strafing. But they were guys from the 1058th. We were lucky."

The officer smiled wrly. "Good. Let's try to keep it that way." He stood up and shrugged. "That's about it, Sergeant. Just keep at it. And watch yourself on your way back up. The Krauts'll start their morning workout any minute now."

Spahn checked his watch. His company commander was right. You could set your watch by the timing of the German artillery bombardment each morning. One was due to hit the American lines—"Here it comes now!" Spahn warned, then ducked instinctively as he heard the whoosh of the high-explosive shell pass over the command post. The tremor shook the building a moment later as the missile from the German 88 struck against the hills behind the town.

The sergeant stuck his helmet on his head and grinned

at the officer. "Well, here goes nothing," he called. Then he threw open the front door and raced out into the teeth of the enemy barrage.

He had almost made it to the bridge when the shell-burst caught him. The explosive hit to his left, about one hundred feet away. Spahn felt the slap of air against him from the explosion; he staggered, clods of earth pelted him and steel fragments whistled by. Then, in a screaming flash of a second, he felt the bite of hot steel in his foot, felt the trickle of warm blood inside his torn combat boot. He toppled to his knees and fell.

A medic was at his side in an instant, slicing away the remnant of his boot, stemming the flow of blood with a compress.

"Take it slow, Sarge," the medic said softly. "Soon as this shelling stops we'll get you back and patch this up. It doesn't look too bad."

Warren Spahn lay in the road near Remagen Bridge and looked at his wounded foot. His first thought was that he was lucky to be alive. Then, he thought back to the time—it must have been ages ago—but no, it was just three short years ago, 1942—yet surely in another world. He had been pitching for Hartford and the Boston Braves had brought him up for a look. He'd pitched only briefly, but had impressed manager Casey Stengel with his style.

He remembered what Stengel had said then. "That Spahn can become one of the best left-handers in the business." Then the manager had added, "If nothing happens to him."

Now, lying there at Remagen, the shrapnel throbbing in his foot, Spahn wondered at the prophecy of Stengel's words. Was this to be it, then? Was his baseball career, barely begun, to end here in the dirt of this foreign town, in a strange country, near a bridge he didn't even know existed a few months ago?

As the medics rolled Staff Sergeant Warren E. Spahn onto a stretcher, in the shadows of Remagen Bridge, who among the most optimistic would have dared predict that the wounded GI would indeed become one of the greatest pitchers in baseball, and would someday lead the Milwaukee Miracle Braves to a World Championship?

Chapter Two ·

Winter loosened its grip on the city of Buffalo reluctantly, and the April afternoon was crisp with the smell of still-melting snows. Warren Spahn, in baggy corduroy knickers and corduroy jacket, raced through the streets, his schoolbooks dangling from a leather strap.

"Pop said he was coming home from work early today so we can practice," he panted to his friend Eddie Basinski, running at his side. "Can you come around?"

Eddie, who would someday play professional baseball with the Brooklyn Dodgers and Pittsburgh Pirates, shook his head. "Not today, Warren. But I'll see you Sunday at the game, right?"

"Okay, Eddie, see you," Warren returned. The two boys separated at the corner, and Warren, still running at top speed, bounded up the steps of his home and charged through the front door.

"Mom! Pop home yet?" he called. He sped through the apartment, shedding his jacket and schoolbooks as he ran. He found his mother in the kitchen. "Hi, Mom," he said as he kissed her. "Pop home yet?" he repeated, breathless and flushed from his exertions.

His mother turned from her cooking to look at him. "I'll bet you don't run that fast getting *to* school," she smiled. "Your father's in the yard, waiting for his all-star first baseman. Or are you a pitcher today? But have a glass of milk first. And don't gulp it down, either."

In the back yard Ed Spahn stood idly tossing a baseball in the air, waiting for his son. He was wearing a baseball cap with the initials "LC" interwound on the peak, and a warmup jacket with Lake City Athletic Club spelled out across the back. Ed Spahn was a wallpaper salesman, and since the year 1930 was not a particularly rewarding one for salesmen, he often found himself getting home early for baseball pratice with his son.

Besides, baseball had always been Ed Spahn's first love. But his slight stature had been against him; he never got past five foot seven and one hundred and thirty-five pounds, and playing third base for the Lake City Athletic Club of Buffalo's semipro Municipal League was as far as his skill and size could carry him.

So Ed Spahn transferred his ambition to his son. As an infant, Warren's first ball was a baseball, and when his father saw the boy pick up the ball and throw it with his left hand, his eyes glowed with anticipation.

"A lefty!" he exulted. "A first baseman! Or a pitcher!"

By the time Warren was old enough for elementary school, daily baseball sessions with his father were the rule during the season. Ed Spahn would rush home from work, grab a big catcher's mitt and make Warren throw to him until it got too dark to see.

"Throw it here, boy," he would coax. "Aim at the mitt. At the mitt. Throw easy—smooth. Atta boy, Warren. Let's see that old follow-through there."

And often—"No! No! Where are you throwing the ball? You're wild! Aim for the mitt. The mitt! You gotta have control. Without control you're nothing! Get that? You're nothing! That's the secret. Control!" he would say fiercely.

And Warren would bite his lip and aim at the mitt. The mitt! Sometimes he could see it in his sleep. The mitt—big and brown and tattered, floating like a leathery moon in his dreams, grinning at him, calling at him— "Aim at me, Warren boy! At me! You gotta aim at me!"

When there was no school, and on Saturdays, Ed Spahn took his son to see the Buffalo Bisons play. Ed knew two men from the International League pro team quite well, pitcher Charlie Perkins, a left-hander who later saw brief action in the major leagues, and first baseman Bill Kelley, who was back at Buffalo after two unsuccessful tries with big league clubs.

Watching the Bisons play, the elder Spahn would say to his son, "Now if you want to be a pitcher, watch every move Charlie Perkins makes. If you want to be a first baseman, watch Bill Kelley." Then, while the game was in progress, he would point out how the players moved around for different hitters and situations; how the first baseman held a runner close to the base, then scampered to his fielding position with the pitch; how he played the position for left-hand hitters and right-hand hitters; how he made the difficult first-to-second and then back to first double play. He pointed out Kelley's technique in playing bunts, catching pop fouls near the stands, all the little things that go into the making of a professional first baseman.

Similarly, when Charlie Perkins pitched, Ed Spahn would say to Warren, "Now watch Charlie's stretch move when there's a runner on first. See how he looks over there to keep the guy from taking too big a lead?" Or, "Now Charlie's got two strikes and no balls on this guy. Watch how he wastes one, then tries to make him bite at a bad pitch. And watch how he moves the ball around—outside, inside, high and low. That's the secret of good pitching, son. And that takes control. Control! Got it?"

Warren Spahn got it. Every afternoon, unless a downpour of rain forced them inside, father and son drilled in the back yard. And the theme was the same: "Control! Aim for the mitt!" The words swam in Warren's head. But he was learning to pitch.

Sunday morning was church time for the entire Spahn family—Mother and Dad, the four Spahn girls and two Spahn boys. But afterward, Warren and his dad were off to the local park, where Ed Spahn played third base for the Lake City Athletic Club. Warren was bat boy for the team, and someday soon he hoped to play for the Athletic Club's midget team.

Now it was April of 1930, and in two weeks—on the twenty-third—Warren Spahn would be nine years old. His father had promised him a new first baseman's mitt for his birthday; because of the friendship that had sprung up between Warren and Bill Kelley of the Bisons, the youngster seemed more favorably inclined toward playing first base than pitching.

So Warren gulped his milk now, despite his mother's admonition, and ran out into the back yard to join his father. "Let's go, Dad," he called. "Throw me a couple of pop flies."

Ed Spahn grinned broadly and tossed a glove at his son. It was a first baseman's mitt, new and dark brown and shiny with oil, redolent of new leather. Warren's eyes bulged as he looked at the glove. He thought it was the most beautiful thing he had ever seen in his life.

"Pop! Gee . . . I mean, this is a beaut! A *real* first baseman's mitt." He slipped his hand into the soft lining and worked his fingers into position. "But you said you might get it for me for my birthday. That's next week. How come you're giving it to me now?"

His father walked over and clapped him on the shoulder. "Can't wait for next week, son," he chuckled. "This Sunday you're playing first base for the Lake City A.C. Midgets."

Warren gasped. "The Midgets! First base! Oh boy!" He jumped up and down and hugged his father. "Pop! You're not kidding me, are you, Pop?"

Ed Spahn laughed. "Kidding? I'll show you if I'm kidding. I'm gonna run you ragged this afternoon fielding grounders and taking my wild throws. When your tongue starts hanging out you'll know I'm not kidding!"

Warren howled. "Bet you call it quits before I do!"

he yelled, and scampered to the end of the yard to start the practice.

For three years Warren played first base for the Lake City A.C. Midgets. But his father was missing no bets. The afternoons were still devoted to practice—not only of the first base position, but pitching as well.

"It's always best to have a little something extra up your sleeve, son," Ed Spahn advised. "You're still young —and you don't know which way the wind's gonna blow yet. It may be that you won't turn out to be much of a hitter, and then you'll never get anywhere as a first baseman. But if you can pitch, you don't have to hit for a hill of beans to make the major leagues."

There never seemed to be much question that reaching the major leagues was the ambition of Ed Spahn for his son Warren. There wasn't any of the usual talk around the Spahn household about Warren's future—no lawyer's or doctor's profession for Warren, no engineering or accounting or teaching post. Baseball, that was it, from the very first.

So Ed Spahn kept shaping his son's pitching skill. The workouts in the back yard continued. "There's no substitute for practice," he said. "Especially to learn control. You got to pitch and pitch and pitch until you can put your foot up on the mound, set yourself, close your eyes and throw a strike right down the middle.

"If you can throw the ball where you want to, son, you can last for years, even when your fast ball's gone."

After three years with the Midgets, Warren began to play with the Casenovia Post American Legion team—

still as a first baseman. The next year he moved up to the Lake City Athletic Club's senior team, where his father was still third baseman. The father-and-son infield combination was the delight of the Municipal League that season; the local fans got quite a kick out of seeing the elder Spahn rifle his swift throws to his slim son at first base.

It wasn't until his first spring at South Park High School that Warren made use of the pitching skill learned so painstakingly in his back yard. When he reported for his first tryout with the high school baseball team, he told the coach he was a first baseman. The coach shook his head.

"To tell you the truth, Spahn," he said to the youngster, "you don't stand much of a chance making the team as a first baseman. We've got Billy Menzerman playing first for us, and Billy was all-scholastic last year. Have you ever played any other position?"

Warren hesitated. "Well . . . I can pitch," he said hopefully.

The coach pursed his lips. "A good pitcher we can always use. Why don't you warm up and show me what you can do?"

Warren trotted off the field, disappointed. He wanted to be a first baseman. But more important, he wanted to play baseball. If he had to make the team as a pitcher, he'd make it as a pitcher, that's all.

He loosened up on the side lines for a while, then reported that he was ready to pitch.

"It's all yours, kid," the coach said, waving at the

pitcher's mound. Then he walked behind the wire-netted backstop to watch the young hurler work.

Warren toed the rubber and looked down at the catcher. He tried to remember everything his father had taught him in the many afternoons of practice. The catcher squatted behind the plate as a batter stepped in to test the pitcher's prowess. Warren licked his lips nervously.

The mitt, the mitt! Aim at the mitt! The thoughts ran crazily through his mind. Control, control! Pitch to spots! Follow through! Snap off that curve! Get hop on that fast ball!

The day was cool but Warren wiped the sweat from his eyes.

He took a deep breath, nodded at the catcher, wound up and burned a fast ball through the middle that popped loudly in the receiver's big mitt. The batter stared—and behind the cage the coach's eyebrows lifted slightly.

Warren came down with another fast ball that zipped by the batter's late swing. The coach leaned in closer to the screen and whispered to the catcher. "Is that kid as fast as he looks from back here?"

The catcher growled back from behind his mask. "All I know is, my hand hurts."

The coach grinned. "Signal for a curve—and let's hope he's got one."

The catcher flicked two fingers in the simple sign for a curve. Warren nodded, coiled in a windup, then spun off a big curve that dipped under the batter's futile swing by six inches.

The coach blinked. "And this kid wanted to be a first baseman?" he muttered to himself. He walked around the backstop and called out to the mound. "Okay, Spahn, now let's see a few without a batter in there. Mix 'em up, fast balls, curves, whatever you got."

For the next five minutes, working easily now with his initial nervousness gone, Warren treated the coach to a dazzling array of fast balls, curves—and pinpoint control.

Finally the coach called a halt to the tryout. He walked out to the pitcher's mound and took the ball from the youngster. "Okay, Spahn, that's enough for now," he said.

Warren drew the sleeve of his sweat shirt across his dripping forehead. "Well, coach, how'd I do?"

The high school mentor smiled. "I think you'll do fine. You have a favorite number you'd like on your uniform?"

A wide grin split Warren's face. "You mean I made the team?"

The coach nodded. "I don't see why not."

"Number thirteen, then," Warren said. "That's the number I've always worn."

"Thirteen, eh? Not the superstitious kind, I see."

"Uh-uh. Thirteen has always been good luck for me."

"Thirteen it is, then. Now let's see you run around the track a couple of times for exercise. And don't fall down," the coach called as Warren raced joyfully for the cinder path that circled the baseball field.

In his sophomore year at South Park High, Warren was a sensation, but it was as a junior and senior that he really got the local baseball addicts talking about him. He was undefeated both years, and capped his uncommonly successful high school baseball career by pitching a no-hit game against Buffalo Tech High.

As delighted as Ed Spahn was with Warren's pitching, so was he unrelenting in his insistence that his son continue to learn. He watched Warren pitch as often as he could, and after each game he was quick to congratulate his son—and equally quick to point out his errors.

"You walked three men, son," he would say. Or, "You had that batter in the eighth inning all set up for the curve. You tried to throw it past him and he belted it." And again, "Listen, son, there are a thousand wild-armed high school kids racking up big strike-out records. It's how many men they walk, though, that counts. To get anywhere, you got to look like a pro, and that means pitching with your head—and control! That's what the big league scouts watch for in a young kid like you—control. If you got a fast ball and can put it where you want it—they can teach you the rest."

And Warren would nod his head and pound his fist into the pocket of his glove. "You're right, Pop. It's just that every once in a while I forget."

"You can't forget, son. Not if you want to be a big league pitcher. A good big league pitcher doesn't make the same mistake twice. Now if you want those scouts to sit up and take notice, you've got to show them that you know what you're doing every minute you're out there."

"Gee, Pop, you really think there are any scouts coming around to our games?"

"Sure there are. They're always hanging around the high school games. Where do you think they find all their young players?" Ed Spahn said. His tone was full of assurance, but there was more hope than conviction in his heart.

However, even Warren's optimistic father couldn't know that those bird dogs of the major leagues—the scouts—were indeed on the trail of the fireballing young left-hander from South Park High. Then, in the spring of Warren's final year at school, while he was warming up before game time, his coach called him over to the side lines.

There was a stranger standing beside the coach, a smiling man who was watching Warren appraisingly as he walked to the bench.

"Warren," the coach said, "this man would like to meet you and talk to you about a couple of things."

The stranger put out his hand. "Hello, Warren. Nice to meet you. What do you say we sit over on one of those benches in the stands where we can talk between ourselves for a while?"

Warren looked at his coach questioningly. "Is it okay, coach?"

The mentor smiled. "I think it might be a good idea. By the way, I forgot to introduce you. Warren, this is Billy Myers."

Spahn shook the man's outstretched hand. "Hello, Mr. Myers."

"Mr. Myers," the coach continued, the smile still playing at the corners of his mouth, "is a scout for the Boston Braves."

Chapter Three ·

Ed Spahn paced the living room of the Spahn home, trying to quell the excitement bubbling within him. "Now let's not everybody get excited," he said, stopping and spreading his hands out before him. "Warren's not pitching for the Boston Braves yet. We've got to talk this thing out quietly and calmly." He resumed his pacing.

The rest of the family sat about the living room, watching as Ed Spahn paced back and forth silently. "The Braves aren't much of a team lately," he said, more to himself than to the rest of them, "but maybe that's an advantage. On some Yankee farm, or even with the Cubs or the Reds, he might get lost in the shuffle. The Braves being so bad lately, they'll probably keep a closer eye on a promising youngster."

"You think that's so, Pop?" Warren chimed in eagerly.

His father looked up, startled, as though suddenly realizing that he had been talking out loud instead of to himself. He stopped pacing. "Well, it's a point to keep in mind. And I like that Myers fellow. He's got a good reputation around Buffalo. In fact, your coach told me that not long ago he was scouting for the Boston Red Sox, but because he didn't like the deal they were offering Sebastian Sisti, some high school kid he found here, he quit them and started scouting for the Braves.

"You can depend on a man like that to give you an honest deal. And that's more important than money. That's something to remember, son."

"Then you think we should sign with Myers, Pop?" Warren asked. It was all he could do to keep from jumping up and down on the living room sofa.

"Well, not so fast, son," his father said. He stood in the center of the room, frowning, rubbing his fingers along the sides of his jaw thoughtfully. Then he shook his head. "No. No, I think you ought to wait, Warren. Finish high school first. Then sign."

Warren felt his stomach turn over with disappointment. He was hurt for the moment, and bewildered, too. Wasn't this what they had been waiting for all these years? Wasn't this the reason for those endless hours of coaching and practice, of throwing a baseball until his fingers blistered and calloused and hardened so that they could break off a curve as sharply as many major league pitchers could?

"I—I don't get it, Pop," Warren said, his eyes misting. "I mean, why wait? Suppose I don't get another chance? Suppose they change their minds by the time I graduate? Suppose . . . suppose anything?" he cried, his voice rising in despair.

"Now listen, son," Ed Spahn said quietly. "I know how you feel. Believe me, I more than anybody know how you feel. I know, because—well, because I know this opportunity, this moment, is something I was waiting for when I was your age—and never got.

"Sure. You want to run out of here and tell every kid in the neighborhood the Boston Braves signed you to pitch for one of their teams. You're proud—and you're happy. And you should be. Darn proud and darn happy. Well don't you think I'm as proud and happy as you are, son?"

Warren just sat there, not answering, looking at the floor at his feet.

"Look at me, Warren," his father pleaded. "Look at me, boy! This is me, your pop! The guy who's been breaking your back for ten years with baseball. The guy who dragged you into the back yard and made you practice pitching like some fathers make their kids practice on a violin! Sure, and you probably hated me for it sometimes —just like those kids!

"But you see what I'm getting at Warren boy," Ed Spahn continued fiercely, his fists clenched tightly at his sides. "I know! I know how you feel because I feel it, too. But there's something else I know, son. And something else I feel. There's more to life and living than baseball." He laughed shortly. "Maybe that sounds funny coming from me. But maybe it's not so funny either. Because when I couldn't make it all the way in baseball, I wasn't prepared for anything else.

"I never got past the sixth grade in school, son," he continued, softer now, "and it shows. What am I? A wallpaper salesman! Warren, I have all the confidence in the world in you. I know—we both know—that you've got the stuff to make the big leagues. But I want you to have one thing first—a high school education. Call it hedging if you want to, but it's something a young fellow's got to have today."

Warren was not quite convinced. However, his father's harangue did serve to lower the pitch of his disappointment. "I don't know, Pop," he said morosely. "I guess maybe I feel this way because I was so sure you'd jump at this chance for me to sign with Mr. Myers. I understand how you feel about my finishing school. But what I'm really afraid of is that the Braves'll change their minds if I don't sign right away."

Ed Spahn shook his head. "Son, if they want you, they'll wait for you. And if they don't want to wait, well, there's plenty of other fish in the sea. And they'll all be around, too, soon as they hear a scout like Billy Myers is after you."

Warren raised his head and looked up at his father. "You really think so, Pop? You really think I'm good enough?"

Ed Spahn walked over to the sofa and put his arm around his son's shoulders. "Think?" he said. "Son, I know it. In here," he said, tapping his chest over his heart. "I'd stake my life on it."

Billy Myers waited for the pitching protégé, as Warren's father had predicted. And when the youngster finished high school the Braves' scout signed him to a contract. Warren's bonus for signing was ample for those days, but today the amount wouldn't buy a major league scout five minutes worth of conversation with a high school star of Spahn's potential.

Warren's parting from his family in the spring of 1940 was a proud and tearful one. As he packed his bags in the room he shared with his brother, his father walked in and stood silently by Warren's bed. Ed Spahn looked down at the clean, worn coverlet and realized how the years had flown by. He remembered when little Warren had first been thought old enough to sleep in a bed of his own, and how the boy's mother worried that he would fall out and hurt himself. "As long as he doesn't fall on his pitching arm," Ed Spahn had joked then.

Warren looked up from his packing and smiled, and Ed Spahn remembered when this slim young man before him had missed the Saturday afternoon movies with the other kids because his father wanted him to learn how to throw a baseball fast and hard and straight.

He remembered, too, the afternoon he'd come across his high school freshman son smoking a crumbling, roll-your-own cigarette in the back yard. He'd offered him one of his own cigarettes from a clean pack and said, "Try a decent cigarette, son. If you like it, smoke it. If you don't, throw it away and forget about them."

Now the boy was a young man, packing to go away and play baseball for a professional team in Bradford, Pennsylvania. And now, too, Ed Spahn realized that in the pressure of teaching the boy how to pitch right, he'd perhaps neglected to teach him how to live right.

"Warren," he began. "Son, I feel as though I've got a

million things to say to you, and darned if I can think of a one right now."

Warren smiled and pressed his hand on his father's shoulder. "I know, Pop. Only you don't have to say them. You've taught me all the important things already. You don't have to worry about me."

The older man nodded. "No, I guess I don't have to worry about you, Warren. You're going to a strange town, gonna live among a lot of different types of men. And you're going to be away from home for the first time in your life. Just remember, son, be a man first, and a baseball player second. When they write things down in the big book Up There, they want to know a man's character, not his profession. Be a gentleman. Have respect for people and they'll respect you. Don't be a loudmouth. Don't get cocky. When you get to Bradford, you'll just be another bush league pitcher trying to beat some other guys out of a job.

"And above all, son," Ed Spahn added, "remember that we're all pulling for you." He took his son's hand and grasped it warmly between his own.

"I know you won't let me down, son."

Warren's face was grim. "I won't let you down, Pop."

That promise was more easily made than kept, however; misfortune rather than any deficiency of Warren's pitching skill made it so. The young hurler reported to manager Jack Onslow of the Bradford Pony League Club full of hope and high spirits. In the clubhouse the first day, he asked Onslow for his favorite uniform number—thirteen.

The grizzled old pilot looked at the clubhouse attendant and jerked his thumb in Warren's direction. "Just what we needed," he said. "A screwball lefty." He turned back to the young pitcher. "Fella, we don't carry any number thirteens. A guy's liable to run into enough tough luck around here without wearing any number thirteen on his back."

Onslow was right about the touch luck, and the unfortunate Spahn got hit by it without wearing the thirteen. In his first twelve games for Bradford, Warren won five and lost four. However, his losses were partly attributable to his teammates' lack of batting support; his earned-run average was a quite creditable 2.73, and he struck out sixty-two men in sixty-six innings pitched, while walking only twenty-four.

Though manager Onslow had seen enough to convince him the youngster had plenty on the ball, Warren was far from satisfied. He began experimenting with a new delivery for an overhand curve. Warming up for a day's game, he snapped the new pitch off too sharply. A lance of flame shot through his left shoulder. He gasped with pain and grabbed at the throbbing joint. Onslow rushed out of the dugout, the Bradford trainer at his heels.

"What's the matter, kid?" the manager asked worriedly. "You hurt your arm just now?"

Warren grinned at Onslow through teeth clenched in pain. "I feel as though my arm's coming off, Skip," he groaned. "My shoulder's on fire."

Onslow sighed wearily. "Better get inside and let the doc here take a look at it. Maybe it's just a little sprain," he said hopefully. "I'll warm up somebody else just in case you can't go today."

The trainer had been probing at Warren's shoulder with practiced fingers while Onslow had been talking. He pressed with his thumbs and Spahn yelped. "Whew," the pitcher whistled. "That hurt, Doc."

The trainer looked at manager Onslow significantly. "This boy won't go today, Jack. He won't go tomorrow, either."

The other man frowned uneasily at the trainer's worried expression. "You think it's bad?" Warren asked.

The trainer shrugged. "I'll want to see X rays first. But don't be surprised if you get a few weeks' vacation out of this."

The gloomy prediction was accurate, unfortunately. Warren had torn several tendons in his left shoulder. "You might as well go home and rest for a few weeks, kid," Onslow told him resignedly. "The doc says you're not to throw a ball until those tendons heal."

Arm in a sling, Warren went home to Buffalo. His father appeared badly shaken by his son's bad luck. "You're sure it's nothing serious, son? Maybe we ought to have some big specialist here take a look at it. Those horse liniment trainers, what do they know—"

"Easy, Pop, easy," Warren interrupted him. "They had regular bone and nerve doctors look me over, taking X rays and the works. I tore a couple of tendons, that's all.

A couple of weeks without throwing and they'll heal good as new."

"A couple of weeks," his father repeated. He ran his hand nervously over his thinning hair and along the back of his neck. He shook his head. "You were only five-and-four when you left. That's not too good. Of course, you dropped a couple of tough ones. They weren't hitting behind you. Still—" He stopped and looked worriedly at Warren. "Well, there's nothing much you can do now but take things easy, like the docs say. Maybe that's all you need, anyway. A couple of weeks back home to get back that old spirit. And when you go back, you'll knock the league on its ear, eh, son?"

Warren grinned at his father. "You bet, Pop."

"That's the talk, son. Meanwhile, maybe we can get out together and watch the Bisons play, like old times. Maybe we can pick up a couple of pointers watching their pitchers while we're at it. They got this guy Freddie Hutchinson pitching for them, used to pitch for the Detroit Tigers last year."

"Sure, Pop," Warren agreed. "That's a great idea."

But two weeks of restless inactivity at home was enough for him. He packed and took the train back to Bradford, his arm still in a sling.

"I think I'm about ready to pitch again," he reported to manager Onslow.

The Bradford pilot glanced dubiously at Spahn's left arm. "Then why the sling?" he inquired mildly.

"I didn't want to take a chance on hurting it again on the train ride down."

Onslow was still skeptical. He understood the impatience of young ballplayers trying to make good, yet he was in need of a good left-hander on his pitching staff. "Okay, Spahn," he shrugged. "But take it real slow at first. I'm not going to start you for at least a week under any circumstances, so don't try to rush back into shape. Just lob the ball around for a couple of days before you try any real throwing."

Warren ducked into the Bradford locker room, removed the sling from his arm and began to suit up. His shoulder was sore and stiff; he could barely bend the arm. "It's just a matter of working out the kinks," he told himself, but slipping on his uniform shirt brought a gasp of pain from his lips.

He trotted out onto the playing field and stood for several moments in front of the dugout, undecided. Then he walked over to the ball bag, took a baseball and waved to one of the Bradford players to throw back and forth with him. Two days later he told Onslow he was ready to pitch batting practice.

The manager squirmed uneasily in his chair. "I don't know, Spahn. Maybe it's too quick. What do you say, Doc?" he turned to the Bradford trainer.

"I can't say—not for sure, anyhow. You just can't tell with these things, Jack. Of course, the safest bet would be to wait at least another week, to let those torn tendons knit more solidly. The X rays show that the scissions have healed. But how strongly . . . ?" He left the question in mid-air.

"You mean we won't know if his shoulder will hold up

until he tries to throw hard, is that it?" the manager questioned.

"At this point, that's about it."

"And if it doesn't hold up? He tears those same tendons again?"

The trainer shook his head. "That won't be so nice. With any fracture or rupture, a second injury on top of the first unhealed one can be darned serious." He looked up at Spahn. "Even permanent."

"What the doc means, Spahn," Onslow explained, "is that you could ruin your arm for good by throwing hard before you're ready."

"But I am ready," Warren insisted. "I've been throwing easily for a couple of days. How will I ever get back into shape if I don't start throwing hard?"

Onslow stood up. "It's your shoulder, fella. I can't tell you if it hurts. You want to pitch batting practice today —go ahead. But soon as you feel one little twinge—you stop. Hear?"

"Right, Skip."

The three men walked out to the playing field together, and while Warren strode to the pitcher's mound, the trainer and the manager stood anxiously next to the batting practice cage.

Spahn tried a couple of soft throws to the catcher, then signaled for a batter to step in and hit . "I'm taking a real workout today," Warren called to his teammate, "so don't expect any soft touches."

With that he stepped resolutely up on the rubber, coiled into a full windup, kicked his right leg high and came down with his first hard pitch since his injury. The split second the ball left his fingers he knew he'd made a mistake. He stumbled forward off the mound and fell to one knee, clutching his left shoulder.

Immediately Onslow and the Bradford trainer were at his side. They picked him up and assisted him into the clubhouse. The trainer probed gingerly with his fingers, watching Spahn's face. The youngster's lips were white; perspiration glistened on his face.

The trainer finished with his examination. "I'm afraid that did it, just as we feared," he announced ruefully. "We'll X-ray it, of course, but there's not much doubt."

Spahn gritted his teeth. "I guess I better take a month off this time, eh, Doc?"

The trainer looked at him balefully. "I think you'll be taking the year off—if you're lucky."

Later, Warren stopped in at the manager's office to say good-by. He shook hands briefly with Onslow and turned to go. The Bradford skipper came around from behind his desk and put his arm around the player's shoulder.

"Tough break, Spahn. The toughest. But go home, take it easy and don't worry. Whenever you get back in shape, your uniform will be here waiting for you."

Warren didn't turn around. "Thanks, Skip," he said brokenly. Then he opened the door and was gone.

Onslow stood for a moment, staring at the door through which the young pitcher had gone, perhaps forever, for all either of them knew. Then he walked around and sat down behind his desk again. He remained there, still staring unseeingly at the door for a long time. After a while he shook his head and laughed sourly.

"You know," he said to the four walls, "maybe I should have given that fella his number thirteen after all."

Chapter Four ·

The Spahn household was immersed in gloom, oppressive, abysmal, impenetrable gloom. The shock of Warren's disabling injury, coming at the very threshold of his major league career, had plummeted the entire family into the depths of melancholy. His father, understandably, took it hardest of all. He fell seriously ill, and when Warren's shoulder healed well enough to do without the sling, the young man went to work to help support the family.

He took a job as a baggage checker at the Buffalo railroad terminal, a task which didn't require that he put great strain on his still-healing shoulder tendons. At night, he rushed home from his job to sit at his father's bedside. He would sit there for hours, talking to the silent figure lying pale and still beneath the white sheets.

"The old wing is getting stronger every day, Pop," Warren would say, forcing the heartiness in his voice. "Soon as you decide you've had enough of this lazing around in bed, I'm gonna put you through a workout in the back yard that'll have you yelling quits. Wait till you catch a couple of my fast ones in that old mitt of yours.

You'll be soaking your hands in cold water for weeks. And listen, Pop, I've been working on a new pitch . . ."

Thus Warren chattered on, his voice eager, but his eyes anxiously searching his father's wan countenance. For often Ed Spahn hardly acknowledged a visitor's presence, but lay staring at the ceiling, unanswering, betraying no sign that he even heard what was being said to him.

There were times when Warren knew he was getting through, however. When he told his father that he'd heard from manager Onslow of Bradford, that the skipper had inquired about Warren's shoulder and said he hoped to see him in camp next spring, it seemed to the youngster that his father's lips had trembled, a tremor of expression had passed briefly over the older man's face.

Then, too, when he talked enthusiastically about his baseball future—which in reality appeared nonexistent at the moment—it seemed to Warren that a light danced in his father's eyes, like the flaring of a match in a darkened room. Like that same match, however, it quickly sputtered and died, leaving the orbs to sit blackly like two dead coals in a waxen mask.

It was these moments of animation that affected Warren more deeply than his father's usual state of indifference. In despair, he sought out the family physician.

"Tell me the truth, Doctor," Warren demanded. "What happened to me—my arm—did that make my father this way?"

"No," the physician returned flatly. "You must not

think that, Warren. True, your father was deeply disappointed at what happened. Hurt, even. I think you're old enough and intelligent enough to understand that your father was unconsciously trying to realize all his aborted baseball ambitions in your success.

"But he was not a well man physically by any means," the physician pointed out. "This, well—breakdown let's call it—might have happened at any time, for any number of similar reasons. No, Warren, it would be morally wrong, in my opinion, to fix the blame for your father's illness on your misfortune."

Warren nodded grimly. "What you're trying to tell me is it's not my fault that it's my fault, isn't that right, Doctor? That my getting hurt was kind of the straw that broke Pop's back?"

The physician frowned. "That's a guilty way of putting it, Warren. Neither you nor your father are guilty of anything but being human beings. And we're every single mortal one of us guilty of that."

Warren sighed deeply. "I don't know, Doctor. I listen to you—and it helps. But it gets to me every once in a while. If there was only something I could do for him!"

"You're doing as much as anybody could do—and that includes me. More than that, well—" the physician shrugged resignedly. "How's your arm feeling these days, Warren?"

"It doesn't hurt, if that means anything. I haven't tried to throw a baseball yet, so who knows?"

"How long must you wait before you try to use it?"

"The club doctors warned me not to try to throw hard

for the rest of the year. And I'm not taking any chances this time. One more rip of those tendons and I can start selling pencils on the street corner."

The physician nodded approval. "Take care of that arm, Warren. It has to carry a load for two good men."

With heavy heart, the youngster left the doctor's office and wandered out into the street. The summer day was dying in a gory smear over the western sky; lights winked on, suddenly, like awakening stars. A breeze picked up the call and sifted through the city, rustling the leaves, spreading in its heady wake the soft sweet scent of the coming night.

Aimlessly, Warren Spahn roamed through the streets, insensible to the sights and the smells and the sounds. He stared at the ground in front of him as he walked, his mind, for the first time in weeks, blessedly devoid of all thought. Thus when he stopped, suddenly, inexplicably, and looked up to see why he had stopped, he was surprised to discover that he was in front of his own house.

Warren climbed the steps wearily, pushed open the front door and walked straight to the bedroom where his father lay. He stood for a moment in the doorway of the room, watching the measured rise and fall of the sheets over the covered form, and he knew his father was asleep. After a while, he stepped to the side of the bed and looked down at the slumbering figure.

"Hold on, Pop," he whispered. "Just hold on till this shoulder of mine heals, till I get another chance. We'll show 'em, Pop. I promise." For a split second the eyelids on Ed Spahn's pallid face appeared to flicker in answer, and Warren felt better. He stood watching several moments longer, then turned away and strode rapidly from the room.

The weeks dragged painfully by, summer turning into fall. Ed Spahn did not improve. Instead, with the first snows of late fall his face grew more pinched and chalky white, his frail body thinner. Then the day came when the Spahn family had to move its bedside vigil to a hospital room. Ed Spahn needed continuous care now.

Warren was nearly frantic with frustration. If only he could tell his father something definite, show him something tangible! But what could he do? He still hadn't tested his shoulder any farther than throwing a hard rubber ball a few feet to one of the neighbor's children. Actually, he felt he didn't want to test the shoulder fully until he got under the hot southern sun during next spring's training—if he was invited to spring training at all, he reflected.

And as maddening as it was for Warren to remain unsure of his baseball future, in truth, he put off testing his shoulder because he was more afraid to know than not to know. Through all the torment of the suspense, he could at least cling to the security of hope.

Finally, the first break came, the first bit of relief in the Spahns' grim battle against illness and despair that began with Warren's injury at Bradford. It was a telegram from the Boston Braves inviting Warren to their next spring training camp in San Antonio, Texas. He read the wire over and over again—he didn't know how many times. Here was something at last! Something he could show Pop! He would read him the telegram, and Pop would understand what it was all about, all right. As soon as he'd hear the words Boston Braves he'd know what it was about.

Warren hugged the precious message to his chest. It wasn't a contract, it wasn't a guarantee, but it was something! They were giving him another chance, and he was certain that under the baking Texas sun his well-rested shoulder would work back into perfect shape.

The weeks following his receipt of the telegram couldn't fly by fast enough for Warren. On the calendar in the Spahn kitchen he had his departing date circled in red, and every night before going to bed he drew a line through another day that brought him closer to San Antonio. Now he bounded into his father's room at the hospital with a new and unfeigned enthusiasm.

As desperately ill as he was, perhaps Ed Spahn perceived that his son's eager air was genuine. There was no sudden change in his critical condition; the telegram did not produce a fairy tale miracle. But by the time there were no more days to cross off before the big red circle on the kitchen calendar, he had been declared out of danger.

The long train ride from Buffalo to San Antonio gave Warren Spahn time to unbend from the strain he had been under for almost a year. For hours he sat gazing out the window at the endless fields, and noticed with the passing hours and miles that the fields changed from white to brown-white to brown and finally to green.

It's like gradually entering into a new world, Warren mused, and maybe how it is with the fields it will be with me. Maybe the cold and the emptiness is behind me, too, and from now on things will be sunny and warm and fruitful.

He smiled to himself at the sentimentality of his thoughts. But he had ample excuse for roseate dreaming; although his father was still in the hospital, he was recovering. And his shoulder?—well, he'd soon know about it.

The Braves' training camp at San Antonio was crowded with scores of players sprawled over several ball fields. In addition to the parent Boston club's players, the camp held men from the Braves' minor league affiliates, and dozens of sandlotters and semipro hopefuls were on hand for tryouts. After the initial settling down period and weeding out of the youngsters who were not quite ready for the pro leagues, the serious work of training, testing and assigning the promising players began.

Of course, the Braves knew all about Warren's shoulder injury and his long siege of inactivity, and they let him take his own time working the joints and muscles loose. But the day inevitably came when the hope had to be replaced by the reality. The Braves had to know whether Spahn could still pitch. If it turned out that he could—fine, he'd get a contract. If his shoulder tore again, or had healed improperly, or Warren had simply lost his stuff—well, the Braves had to know that, too.

It was only batting practice, but when he wound up to throw his first baseball that morning, no one but Warren Spahn knew how much was at stake with every pitch. He threw easily for the first few minutes, lobbing the ball up to the plate to warm up his pitching arm. Then Johnny Cooney, the Braves' outfielder and coach, called to him from behind the batting cage.

"Here we go, Spahn. From now on give it stuff. Make them hit it. Are you ready?"

Warren nodded his assent. He was afraid to trust his voice. His heart pounded and his stomach squirmed and tossed; his hands were clammy with sweat. He wiped his palms across the front of his uniform and stepped up on the mound. He stood there in a kind of paralysis for several moments, staring vacantly at the catcher squatting behind the plate and the batter waving the wood menacingly through the air. The sweat began to trickle down the backs of his legs; he could feel the wetness of his sweat shirt clinging against his skin. So much, so much depended on this next pitch!

For a fleeting second he thought wildly of telling Cooney that he wasn't ready yet, then the shout of the Braves' coach snapped him back to his senses. Cooney had started walking out toward the mound. "Hey Spahn, whatta you say?" he called. "If you're okay, let's go."

Warren shook his head to clear the chilling thoughts and waved Cooney back behind the practice cage. Then he took a deep breath, muttered a silent prayer to himself, coiled his body, kicked his right leg high and let it go—fish or cut bait, pitcher or baggage checker. In an instant, he would know—once and for all.

As he came down in his follow-through, Warren

tensed in anticipation of the first flash of pain through his shoulder. But there was no pain! Not even a twinge! He heard the fast ball pop loudly in the catcher's mitt, and as he took the return throw from the receiver, he had to fight down the temptation to jump high in the air and yell his head off. So far so good. But now that he had that long-feared first pitch behind him, he knew it didn't prove a thing except that his shoulder wouldn't tear apart on the first pitch. He was a long way from home, he realized.

But it was different now. The icy plunge had been taken and withstood. Quickly Warren stepped back on the rubber and fired a second fast ball. The batter swung and missed as the ball smacked into the mitt. A third fast ball—and a third time it slammed into the mitt. Spahn began to pitch in regular rhythm. He uncoiled, his flailing arms going in all directions, right foot pointed at the sky, throwing fast balls that hopped and curves that dipped. Though a trifle wild at first because of his months away from the mound, he gradually narrowed his buckshot serves to the approximate limits of the strike zone.

There was no pain. After six, ten, a dozen pitches, not a sign of pain. When he began to pick off the corners of home plate with unfailing accuracy and the batters began missing more often than hitting, Warren heard Cooney call out for him to stop throwing.

"That's all for you today, Spahnnie. Tomorrow's another day."

Warren bobbed his head to indicate he had heard. He took off his cap, wiped his forehead with the sleeve of his sweat shirt, tucked his glove under his arm and strode off the mound.

On the way to the coolness of the dugout, he passed a cluster of players who had paused in their workout to watch him pitch. All wore Boston Braves uniforms.

"That was nice pitching there, kid," one of the major league regulars said to him.

"Yeah," agreed another. "You looked good out there, busher."

Warren nodded briefly. "Thanks," the nineteen-year-old hurler acknowledged. He continued on toward the dugout, feeling the exultation rising in his throat. The gloom, the despair, the fears dropped from him as he walked, and a fierce joy welled up in his chest and in his eyes. He quickened his pace, bounded down the steps of the dugout and hid his face in the spray of the water fountain.

"This time I won't let you down, Pop," he resolved as the cool stream bathed his dust-caked lips. "This time I won't let you down!"

Chapter Five ·

For all of his years of phenomenal success as manager of the New York Yankees, Casey Stengel still retains the vestiges of his old reputation as a clown. Of course, as boss of the chronically second division Boston Braves in the early 1940's, Casey perhaps found clowning more rewarding than trying to improve his club's perennial seventh place finish. At least he got laughs.

Still, Casey was no less a judge then of potential in a young ballplayer than he is today. And he liked what he saw in Warren Spahn that early spring of 1941. Told of Warren's penchant for wearing number thirteen on his uniform, Casey chuckled.

"That fella can wear number thirteen on his socks for all I care," he said. "If ever a kid looked like a pitcher, this fella's it."

Casey's comment was prompted by two factors. One was that the day before Warren had hurled a two-hitter against the Boston regulars. The other was Warren's pitching form, which was already developing into the perfect, storybook delivery it is today.

The weeks in Texas were indeed sunny ones. Spahn

was rounding rapidly into playing shape, and word from Buffalo was that his ailing father was on the road back to recovery. The future, which had looked so black months before, took on a rosy hue now.

However, Fate still had a couple of tricks left up her sleeve, and it would take Warren several struggling years to shake them loose before beginning his brilliant major league career. As a warning, perhaps, that misfortune was still hanging around hoping to strike a major blow, Warren was involved in a painful accident that spring.

It happened during an exhibition game at Randolph Field, in Texas. He was scheduled to pitch the first few innings of the exhibition, and he was warming up along the first base line, throwing easily to his catcher, while the rest of the Braves' rookies were taking their pre-game infield practice.

"Look out!" The shrill cry of warning split the air.

Warren turned his head toward the sound, just in time to get smacked in the face with a baseball that had been thrown wildly from the infield. He sank to his knees with a sharp gasp of pain and surprise, his hands covering his face. Blood gushed angrily from his nostrils, splashing his hands and the front of his uniform. In a moment he was surrounded by his teammates, and the Braves' trainer was examining the injury.

The player who threw the errant baseball was frantic with anxiety. "I hollered for him to look out," he explained, his voice pleading. "The throw got away from me. I hollered, but I guess he didn't hear me."

"Don't worry about it," Spahn managed to groan, his

lips compressed tightly in pain. "It was my fault. I should have ducked."

The trainer looked up from his examination of Warren's nose. "Let's stop the gabbing and get this guy in the clubhouse," he said. "Carry him in, and keep his head tilted back. He's got some beaut of a broken nose there."

In the clubhouse, the trainer applied ice packs to Spahn's nose and cheekbone areas, which were rapidly swelling to balloon-like proportions. Finally the hemorrhaging stopped, but the trainer shook his head worriedly.

"We better get him to a hospital to have that thing looked at. I can't do anything here about that broken nose."

They couldn't do much for Warren at the hospital, either. He had two black eyes and a broken nose, but all that could be done was treat the areas with iced compresses and hope the broken bone in his nose would set itself properly.

When Spahn showed up on the ball field several days later, wearing sun glasses to hide the still purplish-black bruises around his eyes, he was the subject of much good natured kidding from his teammates.

"Hey, who hung the shiner on you, kid?" came from the veterans on the Braves.

"Don't try to tell us you walked into a door."

"Hey, who's the movie star with the dark glasses?"

But as the days wore on, it was Warren's nose that really caught the needling eyes at the training camp. The broken bone had healed crookedly, leaving him with an oversized, misshapen appendage that became the target for all the camp wits.

"Look at the Great Profile," one of them said derisively, comparing Spahn's battered visage with the classic features of the original Great Profile, the late actor John Barrymore.

"Get a load of the hook on that guy," came another teasing comment.

Warren took it all with a patient grin, knowing full well the penchant ball players have for kidding each other, and realizing, too, how unpopular is the player who can't take the friendly bantering. And one concrete thing the kidding did accomplish. It provided him with a nickname. He was so utterly devoid of the idiosyncrasies ball players usually pick on to nickname each other, that as a result of his bulging nose he was soon dubbed "The Profile" and "Hooks." The names are still with him.

When the 1941 season opened, Warren was shipped off to Evansville, Indiana, in the Three-I League. Here, for once, he ran into double good fortune: Evansville's manager was a patient, understanding, able teacher named Bob Coleman, and Warren's roommate was a youngster named Willard Donovan, a pitcher who never could make the grade with Boston, but deserves honorable mention in Braves' archives for his role in Spahn's career.

Donovan may not have been much of a pitcher when it came to throwing at home plate, but he had the best move toward first base in the business—at least he did until Warren Spahn learned it and added a few extras of his own. During their year together as roomies with Evansville, the two young hurlers spent many hours discussing Donovan's method for holding a base runner on first, and picking off the careless ones.

On afternoons when neither hurler was due to work, Donovan would practice the technique with Warren, unselfishly imparting to his friend the one major league skill he had in his pitching repertoire. How well Donovan taught Spahn is evident by the respect base runners have had for Warren down through the years. Hardly anyone ever tries to steal second on Spahn; the only player who has done it with any degree of success is Pee Wee Reese of the Dodgers who, percentagewise, is probably the best base stealer in baseball.

Young speed demons, breaking into the National League, inevitably have to learn about Spahn the hard way, despite even veteran umpire Babe Pinelli's admonition that "Spahn has the greatest motion toward first base I have ever seen." One such embarrassed base-running flash was Jackie Robinson, undoubtedly one of the fastest in baseball history—and, in his rookie year, 1947, the league's base-stealing champ.

Jackie quickly learned about Spahn. In the first game they faced each other, Warren picked him off first base —twice.

Spahn had a great season at Evansville. He led the league with a 19–6 record, had one hundred and ninety-three strikeouts and an earned-run average of 1.83. He hurled seven shutouts, ran up a string of forty-two consecutive scoreless innings at one point, and pitched three one-hit games.

It was a triumphant return to Buffalo for Warren. The previous year's miseries were all but forgotten; the family spoke eagerly of what lay ahead for him in baseball. The Braves had finished seventh, for the third straight year, which was no unimportant factor in the family's thinking.

"They might even bring you up next season, Warren," ventured his father, in better spirits than he had been in since his son's high school baseball days. "Why, you're better now than half of those crumbs on the Braves ever will be."

Warren grinned. "I hope Casey Stengel agrees with you, Pop."

"Well if he doesn't, he's crazier than they say he is," Ed Spahn growled.

Of all the things Casey Stengel might have been in those years, one of them was not crazy. Of course, while piloting the inept group of players that made up the 1941 Boston Braves, Stengel was often given to eccentricities which were more demonstrations of his frustration than anything else. On several occasions when it seemed to Casey that the umpires were allowing extra inning games to drag on into near darkness, he showed his displeasure by signaling to his bull pen with a flashlight.

But Stengel was not crazy. He knew what the Braves needed—new, young, talented ballplayers. Men like Warren Spahn. But where to get them? Boston had been lucky with Spahn, partly because of scout Billy Myers's persuasive efforts. But Stengel knew that in order to attract young talent, the Braves needed new blood, new organization, new money. Not many Boston fans were willing to pay for the doubtful pleasure of watching the Braves in action. In fact, the joke among the local baseball writers was that if the many Braves stockholders came out to the park on the same day, they would outnumber the paying customers.

So Stengel did the best he could with what he had. And in the Braves' spring training camp of 1942, he had a pair of young pitchers destined to give Boston a pennant in 1948. But by the time "Spahn and Sain, and pray for rain" became as famous in Boston as "One if by land, two if by sea," Stengel was long since gone from the scene.

The friendship that blossomed between Warren Spahn and Johnny Sain in 1942 had all the appearances of a mutual admiration society. Sain was four years older, but the first time he saw Spahn pitch in spring training, he was openmouthed in astonishment.

"Where'd you learn to pitch like that?" he asked. "Man, I'd give anything to have form like that!"

Warren laughed. "Tell you what, I'll trade you. My form for your curve ball," he said to Sain, whose curve was indeed something to behold.

Sain was not the only pitcher to marvel at Warren's picture delivery. Because the outbreak of World War II several months before had curtailed railroad travel, the Braves trained in Sanford, Florida, that spring, and played most of their exhibition games in that area. One day in Tampa, Spahn was working against the Cincinnati Reds, when Bucky Walters, their pitching ace, asked a Boston baseball writer, "Who is that guy out there, anyway?"

The writer shrugged. "Some kid." He checked his notes. "Name's Spahn. Warren Spahn. Did pretty good with Evansville last year."

Walters grunted in surprise. "He may be a kid, and he may turn out to be a two-bit pitcher, but that delivery of his alone is worth ten thousand dollars."

Strangely, it was something in Spahn's impressive delivery that was responsible for his unimpressive beginnings in the major leagues. The man who spotted it—and gave away his advantage by boasting about it—was Charlie Dressen who coached the Brooklyn Dodgers in 1946. After Brooklyn had shellacked Spahn one day, Dressen gloated, "We can beat Spahn every time he pitches." And then he made the mistake of telling why. But that wasn't to be until 1946. In 1942, Spahn's delivery was not only beautiful to behold, but considered flawless.

Toward the end of the 1942 exhibition tour, when Coach Johnny Cooney told Spahn he would open the season with the Braves, Warren wanted to dash off and call home about the exciting news. But Cooney cautioned him first.

"I don't want to sound like a kill-joy, Warren," the coach said. "I know what a big thing this is for you and your folks. But if you look at this thing the way it honestly is—why, you don't get hurt if you get shipped down again."

Spahn stared at him. "Shipped down?"

Cooney shrugged. "Listen, Warren, you know every club brings up a whole lot of extra guys when the season opens, especially pitchers, just for a quick look. Then they send them down to a farm team when June comes around and the rules say a team can't carry more than twenty-five men."

"Is that what Casey's bringing me up for, a quick look?"

"Maybe quick, maybe long; it depends on a lot of things," Cooney replied. "One of them will be how many pitchers we lose to the Army by June. Like I said, Warren, I don't want to be a kill-joy. But I've seen kids get all busted up because they thought they were no good when they got shipped back down. I figured a guy like you would want to know the score."

Warren appeared thoughtful for a moment. Then he nodded his head. "Yes, I guess you're right, Cooney. It's better that a guy should know. Sure. Then, if he expects it, he's not so disappointed. And if he makes the team—well, it's all the bigger thrill, I guess."

Whether Cooney had advance knowledge of what was planned for Spahn, or whether he was speaking from general experience, he called the turn. Warren was sent to Hartford after appearing briefly in two unimportant relief roles. Some baseball followers have claimed that manager Stengel was too quick to sour on Spahn, since both of the pitcher's efforts were unimpressive. However, it was more probable that Casey saw little use in subjecting an inexperienced twenty-year-old to the beatings he might have taken with the ineffectual Braves.

He gave Warren the news himself. "Spahnnie, you're only twenty years old . . ." he began.

"Twenty-one," Warren interrupted. "Last week."

Stengel grimaced. "Not a very happy birthday present we got for you, is it, kid? But like I was telling you, you're only twenty years old—okay, twenty-one—" he held up his hand as Warren started to protest the error—"and you got plenty of years ahead of you. A young pitcher like you needs a lot of work, and you wouldn't get much of that on this club. Besides, with some of them lummoxes playing with you, you wouldn't be winning many games. Next thing you know, you'll think something's wrong with your pitching, and you'll get to fiddling around with new pitches and all, and before you know it you'll have killed that million-dollar form of yours."

Along with Spahn, the Braves sent to Hartford Willard Donovan, who had also had a brief look with the Braves. The two men roomed together again, and Donovan resumed coaching Warren in the pick-off motion.

Spahn had won seventeen and lost twelve at Hartford, with an excellent 1.96 earned-run average, when the call came, at the tail end of the 1942 season, to report back to the Braves. He started two games, did not finish either one and received no decisions. His brief visits with the Braves were not ones to portend bright things for Warren's future; he had a poor earned-run average of 5.63, giving up ten runs and twenty-five hits in sixteen innings of pitching. What's more, his vaunted control was not in evidence—he struck out seven and walked eleven.

Nevertheless, Stengel saw beyond the statistics. Sitting in the Boston dugout one morning before a game, Casey nodded toward Warren who was warming up along the first base line. "That fella," he said to a Boston baseball writer, "someday he's going to be one of the best left-handers in the league." Then Casey, perhaps thinking of the war, or of his own hard luck managing the Braves, muttered gloomily the phrase that Warren was to read in the papers next day and then recall three years later as he lay wounded at Remagen Bridge in Germany.

"That is," Stengel said, "if nothing happens to him."

Several months later, Casey's words took on their more ominous portent. Warren was drafted into the United States Army.

Chapter Six ·

Warren E. Spahn, buck private, Army of the United States, stood in the predawn blackness of Camp Gruber, Oklahoma, and shivered in the penetrating cold, made even more marrow chilling by his sleepiness. Although he had experienced cold in Buffalo, never had he been forced to leap out of a warm bed at the blast of a bugle, and in two minutes rush fully dressed into the street. There was something unnerving about the experience.

All along the company street at Camp Gruber, men were flying madly out of barracks' doors to join the groups lined up in shivering rows for morning roll call. They stood alike in their long, shapeless khaki overcoats, hands stuffed into pockets, shoulders hunched, staring straight ahead with glazed, sleep-lidded eyes.

"Wh-who needed this?" Warren Spahn stuttered through chattering teeth. "I could be living like a king in Florida now, in the warm sun."

The soldier next to him, a friend of his from Buffalo named Roy Reimann, laughed derisively. "Gowan, you never had it so good," he scoffed with the GI's favorite wartime phrase.

"Shaddap in there!" bawled the platoon sergeant.

The shivering GI's hunched deeper into their coat collars.

That evening, with the day's grueling training done, the exhausted soldiers lay on their cots in the barracks, many of them, after months in the Army, still wondering how they got there and what it was all about. Often the whole thing seemed like a dream. Some of the GI's sat and smoked and talked about home; some wrote letters, others sat around on foot lockers listening to the GI who was part of every barracks in every camp in the United States during the war—the GI who played a guitar and sang hillbilly songs. The guitar player in Warren Spahn's barracks was going through his second chorus of "Take me back to Tulsa, I'm too young to marry," when Roy Reimann suddenly sat upright on his cot.

"Hey, Warren," he called to Spahn, whose bunk was directly across the room, "that reminds me—you coming into Tulsa with me Friday night?"

"Sure thing, Roy. Brooksie going to fix us up with one of her home cooked dinners?"

"I hope so. Y'know, I can't figure out whether Brooksie's really a good cook, or she's only good compared to what I get here all week long," Roy reflected.

Warren laughed. "Don't try to figure it out. It's liable to break up a beautiful marriage."

His buddy chuckled. "Yeah. And listen, speaking about marriage, when are you and Lorene gonna get hitched?"

Warren smiled wistfully. "Oh, I don't know, Roy.

We've been talking it over pretty seriously—and just about decided to wait till I get back from overseas."

A GI sitting on the bunk next to Spahn's paused in the process of shining his shoes. "You mean *if* you get back from overseas," he interjected.

Reimann grimaced at the man. "One of the happiness boys," he said.

"Trouble is, mopey Joe here is right," Warren said somberly. "I mean, who's kidding who, Roy? They feed us all the fancy statistics in the lectures about doing the job right and coming back—but look around the barracks. Some guys here probably won't come back. How do I know one of them won't be me?"

Reimann sighed wearily. "Sure, that's the logical way to look at it, Warren, but I don't know—the way I figure it, you gotta take the chance. I mean, you can't just stop living just because you're in the Army and might get killed someday. It, well, it doesn't seem right, that's all."

"I know what you mean, Roy," Spahn replied thoughtfully. "But still it doesn't seem right to me to make a girl worry about being a widow before she's even had a chance to be a wife."

The GI shining his shoes stopped again. "Yeah, and how about a guy coming back with a piece of him missing?"

Reimann threw his metal helmet liner at the GI. The man ducked and laughed. Roy shook his head. "Hey, you sure the Nazis didn't smuggle you in here to kill our morale?"

"Who could kill your morale?" the GI hooted. "You two chow hounds found a home in the Army!"

The three of them laughed together then. In a few moments, the lonely notes of taps sounded and the camp was locked in darkness. On his iron cot, Warren lay staring upward into the blackness, thinking.

Meeting Lorene Southard had made everything else about the Army worth the discomfort. She was a bright girl, the confidential secretary to the president of an oil company. He had met her through Roy; she shared an apartment in Tulsa with Brooksie, Roy's wife. Warren hadn't been particularly eager to accompany Roy when his friend had told him about Lorene, mostly because of his feelings about the uncertainties of the future of a combat engineer.

But he and Lorene had hit it off from the very beginning, and before long they had found themselves discussing the advisability of getting married. Torn by arguments that were facing servicemen and their girls all over the country, Warren and Lorene had finally decided to wait. It was a painful decision for both of them, but lying there in the darkness of his barracks, Warren knew that before many more days would pass, he would be on his way overseas. To what? he wondered, and sighed aloud.

The pessimistic GI in the next bunk turned his head. "Say, Spahn," he whispered, "I was really only kidding before. I really think it's okay to marry the girl, if you want to."

Warren smiled in the darkness. "I know," he said. "Thanks."

"Knock it off, you guys," growled a voice near by. "We got a hard day tomorrow."

In the summer of 1944 Spahn was shipped overseas, a sergeant now in the 276th Engineer Combat Battalion. With units of all types that had been gathered from camps throughout the country, the 276th was attached to the main fighting force of the 9th Armored Division. Together, they slipped silently out of New York Harbor on the *Queen Mary*, bound for Scotland. Near the end of October, the green troops were sent into the front lines in Belgium, near Luxembourg, a quiet section of the line. But it wasn't quiet for long.

Out of the foggy bleakness of the morning of December 16, 1944, German Panzer troops stormed into the American positions in their last desperate offensive of the war. Thus began the historic Battle of the Bulge. A week later the battered units of the 9th Armored were pulled out for a rest; they had lost heavily in men and equipment, but their stubborn resistance had helped break the back of the German attack. For his valorous part in the Battle of the Bulge, Staff Sergeant Warren E. Spahn was awarded a Bronze Star medal.

Three months later the division was at Remagen, and Warren Spahn's engineers were working under shellfire and bombardment to repair the damaged span over the Rhine—the only bridge the Allied armies had been able to capture intact along the entire length of the river.

Then, that fateful morning of March 17th, the German artillery shell came close to ending it all for Warren.

Fortunately—if anything about a battle wound can be considered fortunate—the shrapnel in Warren's left foot left no permanent effects. He continued on into Germany with his division until V-E Day. Several months later, in recognition of his leadership under fire during the war in Europe, Spahn was commissioned a second lieutenant in the Corps of Engineers.

Nearly a year of occupation duty followed for Warren —not a leisurely time, either, for the engineers were busy repairing roads and bridges for the use of the occupying armies. But the danger was over—and except for the fitful dreams filled with exploding shells and the cries of the wounded, the days of battle were forgotten.

As the winter of 1945 turned into the spring of 1946, Warren's impatience to return to civilian life was rapidly being matched by two other people in his life—John Quinn, general manager of the Boston Braves, and Billy Southworth, the team's new manager.

After a number of successful years with the St. Louis Cardinals, Southworth had been hired to dig the Braves out of their second division rut. The prospect didn't appear encouraging. But talking to reporters that spring in the Braves' training camp at Fort Lauderdale, Florida, he painted the picture as brightly as he could.

As the Boston pilot enumerated the assets of his team, the baseball writers nodded their heads patiently; they were used to spring briefings filled with rose-colored clichés and hollow promises.

Finally one of the writers broke in. "Yeah, but how about your pitching, Billy?"

"Well," Southworth returned, "how about it?"

"Who've you got?"

Southworth, notoriously poor on names, pondered for a moment. "Well, we've got Johnny Sain, and what's-his-name, who we got from the Cardinals—Cooper. Mort Cooper. And Ernie White. And then we got this guy coming out of the Army any day now. Spahn. Warren Spahn. We got good reports on him from Bradford and Hartford. We expect a lot of good things from Spahn this year."

"Spahn?" the reporter repeated. "I think I remember him. Tall, lanky kid. Had a nice move. Had a sore arm a while back, I think."

The manager winced. That's all he needed, a sore-armed pitcher. Ernie White was the only other left-hander on the team, and the Braves needed Spahn desperately. "I understand Spahn's all over that now," he said hopefully.

"Will he be getting out of the Army in time for opening day?" someone asked.

Southworth spread his hands. "Your guess is as good as mine. You know the Army. However, we've been in touch with his fiancée in Tulsa, and she'll notify us as soon as she hears he's on the way back from Europe."

The weeks passed and the Braves received no word from Warren. The season opened—and still no Spahn. Then, in Tulsa one evening, Lorene Southard was just sitting down to dinner when the doorbell rang. "Now who can that be?" she said aloud to herself. She strode briskly across the room and opened the door. A startled cry escaped her lips.

"Warren!" she gasped.

"Surprise!" Spahn cried. He swept Lorene off her feet and carried her into the room. "Surprise! Surprise!" he kept shouting as he swung her around in his arms.

"Warren! Warren!" she laughed and cried at the same time. "Put me down!"

The two of them fell onto the sofa in a laughing tangle. Flushed and breathless with joy and excitement, Lorene finally managed to blurt out her surprise. "How did you get here? Why didn't you call me?" she asked.

Warren laughed. "For three years I've been promising myself that when the great day came I wasn't going to call or anything. Just calmly walk up to your door, ring the bell and say, 'Honey, I'm home.' So—I'm home."

"Good," Lorene said. "And you're just in time for dinner."

Warren surveyed the neatly arranged table and sighed. "Food. Real food. On a real table with knives and forks and dishes. It's been a long time."

Later, relaxing over his second cup of coffee, Warren said suddenly, "By the way, honey, I don't suppose anybody from the Braves has been asking about me, have they?"

"Asking about you!" Lorene exclaimed. "That's all they've been doing is asking about you. Every day for weeks they've been annoying me with phone calls—asking me when you're coming home."

Warren leaned forward excitedly. "No kidding!" he exulted. "Boy, I was worried that they'd forgotten about me altogether." He leaned back in his chair. "Calling every day, eh? Who called? What did he say?"

"It was a Mr. Quinn, the manager or something."

Warren smiled. "He's general manager. There's quite a difference."

Lorene waved her hand. "Well, anyway, he's been calling me every day, telling me some complicated story about the troubles the Braves are having, and how important it is that you join the team as soon as you come home. Now isn't that ridiculous?"

Warren ignored the last remark for the moment. "What kind of trouble was Quinn talking about?" he asked.

"Oh, I don't know. You know how little I know about baseball. Something about their being in sixth place, whatever that is, and some left-handed fellow has a sore arm, things like that."

Spahn's eyes widened. "Ernie White has a sore arm?"

"Yes, that's the name he mentioned," Lorene said. "That Ernie fellow. Anyway, Mr. Quinn seemed to think that it was terribly important, and he told me that whenever you got here I was to tell you to call him right away."

Warren got up and headed for the telephone. "Well, I will call him, right now."

"Warren!" Lorene's sharp cry stopped him.

"What is it, honey?"

"Warren, you haven't been home more than half an hour. You're still wearing your Army uniform—and yet you're ready to put on your baseball uniform at a moment's notice and go to work?"

Warren looked at her, surprise evident on his face. "But Lorene, this is what I've been waiting for. It's a great spot for me. The team needs me. I've been worried that I'd get lost in the shuffle somewhere, and here I come home and find out the Braves can't wait to get me back. Don't you see what a great opportunity this is for me to show what I've got?"

"But Warren," Lorene protested, "what about our plans to get married as soon as you got back, to go away somewhere quietly for a while—to help you forget these last three years?"

"Honey, the minute I get a uniform on and get out there on the mound in a ball game, I'll forget there ever was such a thing as a war."

Lorene sighed. "Well, it was nice to dream about being a June bride, anyway."

Warren picked up the phone. "We can still get married in June. But in Boston." He dialed long distance. "I hope he's home now," he said, half to himself.

"He's in Pittsburgh," Lorene said, defeat in her voice. "He called me from there this morning."

Warren smiled. "Don't worry, honey, everything's going to be—oh, operator, I want to make a person-to-person call to Mr. John Quinn in Pittsburgh. That's right, Quinn . . ."

Three hours later—four hours all told since he returned home from the Army—Spahn was on his way to Pittsburgh to rejoin the Braves. Quinn had gone all out in persuading him to join the team at once—a substantial increase in Warren's meager prewar salary was promised, and to placate Lorene, the Braves general manager had offered to pay for the Spahns' wedding and honeymoon.

"Why, we'll even get Billy Southworth and his wife to stand up for you," Quinn told Warren on the phone.

Lorene reluctantly agreed to meet Warren in Boston.

"You'll see," he said to her as he boarded the train for Pittsburgh, "everything's going to work out fine. You'll like Boston."

But Lorene didn't like Boston. She arrived several nights later in the midst of a drenching rain. The Braves were still out of town, in New York, not due back in Boston for two more days. After a lonely, sleepless night in a hotel room spent listening to the clattering of the rain against the windows, Lorene had had enough. The next morning she called Spahn in New York.

"Warren, I'm going home," she told him abruptly.

"Home!" Spahn was stunned. "But you just got there. What are you going home for? I don't understand, Lorene."

"Oh, I'm just so miserable, Warren," she wailed. "This is no good. What am I going to do here? I'm so lonesome. I don't know anybody in Boston. All I do is sit by myself in my hotel room and look out the window."

"But I'll be there in two days, honey. You can stick it out for two days," Spahn urged.

"No, I can't. And what happens when you get back? You'll stay for a while and then go away again and leave me here not knowing a soul."

"Gee, honey, I thought we'd get married when I got to Boston."

"No, Warren. I don't want to get married at second base or some place like that—and eat hot dogs on our honeymoon. No, I've thought it all out and I think we'd better postpone getting married until the baseball season is over."

Warren's arguments and protestations were in vain. Lorene had made up her mind, and immediately after talking to him she checked out of her hotel and left for Tulsa.

It was a dejected and much-abashed Warren Spahn who pulled into Boston two days later with the Braves. Some of the gloss was gone from the bright picture as he had seen it not so many days before—coming back to the Braves, Lorene with him here in Boston, getting married.

But Lorene wasn't here, and the city seemed cold and empty without her. What was more, he hadn't as yet done any pitching for the Braves. Since he joined the team in Pittsburgh he had done nothing but work his arm back into shape by pitching batting practice and serving time in the bull pen.

He was ready now, but manager Southworth showed no inclination toward letting him into a game. A series with the St. Louis Cardinals went by, and still Warren toiled on aimlessly in the bull pen. Then Chicago came into town. The opening game in the series was a night game, a popular innovation at Braves Field that year. When the game began Warren took his glove and strolled out to the bull pen. He deposited himself on a bench there and breathed deeply of the night air. Warren liked this night game business. The air was fresh and cool. He reflected that his fast ball would be a lot harder to hit under the lights.

As usual, the Braves were not in good form that night. Behind the stalwart pitching of their ace Claude Passeau, the Cubs were coasting along on an 8–0 lead. As was his custom in the middle innings of a ball game, Warren was warming up easily, just to keep his arm limber. It was the top of the seventh inning. The first Cub batter walked. The next one singled. Billy Southworth trudged out to the mound, waving his left arm at the bull pen. Idly watching the proceedings, Warren paid little attention to Southworth's beckoning arm.

Finally, one of the umpires had to fetch him. The arbiter ran halfway out to the bull pen and called him. "Let's go, Spahn, you're holding up the game."

Only then did Warren realize that Southworth was calling on him to pitch. Startled, he called back to the umpire. "Me?" he shouted.

"Your name's Spahn, isn't it? C'mon, let's get going."

Warren could barely suppress his excitement. He walked stiff-leggedly nervous, across the green expanse of the outfield, the din of the crowd in his ears rhythmic and far away, like the sound of the ocean's roar heard in a seashell. He scuffed at the dirt of the infield and strode to the mound. Southworth stood there, calm and distant, juggling the baseball in his hand. When Warren reached him he plunked the ball into the pitcher's glove and patted him on the arm. "It's all yours," he said, and stalked back into the Braves dugout.

Spahn finished his warm-up tosses and nodded to catcher Phil Masi that he was ready. Then he drew a deep breath, stretched, checked the base runners and threw a strike past Cub shortstop Lenny Merullo, the first major league batter he had faced since the fall of 1942.

The crowd roared. Manager Southworth sat watching indifferently. Feeling more assured with that first pitch out of the way, Warren settled down to business. He whistled another strike past Merullo, wasted a pitch for a ball, then struck out the Cub batter on a fast curve that dipped below his flashing bat.

Warren turned his back on home plate and exulted. Those pitches felt good. He rubbed the ball between his palms as he gazed vacantly at the Braves' outfield, then he turned around and went back to work. The next batter was pitcher Claude Passeau. Warren fanned him on three pitches. Southworth sat up abruptly in the dugout. Stan Hack, the Cubs' dangerous lead-off man, stepped into the hitter's box. Spahn went into his stretch, looked back at the runners, kicked high and threw to the plate. Hack swung and missed. Spahn's next pitch was a ball, then a strike that curved away from the left-handed batter. Warren came back with his fast ball. Hack swung and trickled the pitch to the mound. Spahn pounced on it, flipped to first—and the side was retired.

Warren touched the peak of his cap as he strode back to the dugout, acknowledging the applause from the stands. "Nice goin'," Southworth grunted. Spahn mopped his face with a towel. The Braves went down in order and he popped quickly out of the dugout to pitch the eighth inning.

Cub second baseman Don Johnson fouled to catcher Masi. Peanuts Lowrey grounded out to second base and Phil Cavaretta struck out. Six Cubs up, six down. In the Braves' dugout, manager Southworth watched keenly now.

In the ninth, Warren gave it all he had, anxious to make an impression this first time out. He struck out Andy Pafko and the dangerous Bill "Swish" Nicholson. The crowd was yelling now with each blazing pitch, each futile swing of the bat. And Warren struck out Cub catcher Mickey Livingston. Southworth was standing at the edge of the dugout, eyes glittering. When it was over, Warren stuck his glove in his pocket and strode proudly off the mound.

Spahn starred in relief several more times before Southworth gave him a starting assignment in Brooklyn. The Dodgers promptly knocked him out of the box, though the Braves eventually got him off the hook by winning the game, 8–5. This was the beginning of a peculiar history of ineffectiveness at Ebbets Field for Warren, an ineffectiveness so marked that eventually it was to become a Braves' practice never to pitch Spahn in Brooklyn.

Boston went over the river to play the Giants next, and Spahn lost his first major league game. Then he got hot and won five straight. But he wasn't happy. As the Braves hopped about the country, Warren was spending more time in phone booths than on the mound. Almost daily he called Lorene in Tulsa, where she was now feeling more miserable than she had in Boston. Spahn kept asking the Braves for a few days off to get married, but he was in the middle of his winning streak, and manager Southworth didn't want to break his pitcher's routine with distractions like getting married.

"After the season," the Braves' pilot put him off. "Then we'll stake you to the wedding and a big honeymoon."

But in August matters came to a head. Lorene had been moping around her office for weeks. She was sitting at her desk, staring longingly out the window one day, when her employer approached her.

"Listen, Lorene," he said kindly, "this can't go on. You're not doing your work properly here, and I'm sure your young man can't be doing his right, either. Either marry him—or forget him."

Lorene had no intention of forgetting Warren; she quit her job next day and flew to Boston. Confronted by the determined faces of both Spahn and his fiancée, the Braves gave in. As promised, they made plans for a big wedding for the couple, but at the last minute Warren and Lorene slipped away and were married quietly.

General Manager John Quinn greeted the newlyweds on their return. "That promise to pay for your honeymoon still holds," he said. "Lorene can come along on the next road trip, at our expense."

However, now that everything on the domestic front

had been smoothed out for Warren, matters became stormy on the pitcher's mound. He lost his next four games in a row. Two of the four losses were to the Dodgers, and after the last defeat Brooklyn coach Charlie Dressen chortled, "We can beat Spahn every time he pitches." Then Dressen gave away his secret by boasting, "We know every pitch he throws."

Warren won his next three games, to finish the season with an 8–5 record, and a quite creditable 2.93 earned average. Nevertheless, Dressen's boasting rankled him, and in the spring of 1947 he got together with coach Johnny Cooney in an attempt to eliminate this flaw in his pitching delivery. Warren realized there could be no success for a pitcher who "telegraphs" his pitches—that is, tips off enemy batters to what he's going to throw because of differences in his motions. Obviously, a batter knowing that a fast ball is coming up, or a curve ball, can prepare himself, follow and time the pitch perfectly. An important part of a pitcher's success lies in his ability to fool the batter and keep him off balance.

Spahn and Cooney worked on three phases of his pitching. First, his already smooth delivery was made flawless; every motion, whether for fast ball or curve, was alike. Secondly, they practiced concealing pitches from the coaching boxes, for astute coaches, watching a pitcher grip the ball during the windup, can flash a sign to the batter what kind of pitch to expect. And third, Cooney worked with Warren on developing a slow curve, an extra pitch which would serve to change the pace off his fast ball and fast curves. When the 1947 season opened, Warren was more confident than he had ever been before.

Things were looking up for the Braves, too, in 1947. They had finished fourth under manager Southworth the year before, their first finish in the first division since 1934, when they had also finished fourth.

During the winter the Braves had picked up third baseman Bob Elliott from the Pirates, and brought up a brash young first baseman from Seattle, Earl Torgeson. Johnny Sain had won twenty games in 1946 and Spahn had looked good in spots. Boston fans, who for years had been giving most of their business to the Red Sox at Fenway Park, began to take new interest in their National League representatives.

Warren started the 1947 season as though he would never be beaten. And, in truth, with better support behind him, it is possible that he might not have been. He reeled off eight straight wins in the first month of the season, then lost the ninth when center fielder Johnny Hopp misplayed a routine fly ball into a triple. It was a bad break that would have sent many a pitcher into a tirade of anger or self-pity. Not Warren Spahn.

In the Braves' clubhouse after the game, he approached the unfortunate Hopp, who was sitting disconsolately on a stool in front of his locker. Warren tousled the outfielder's hair and punched him playfully in the shoulder. "Forget it, Johnny," he said. "If we hadn't lost it one way, we'd have lost it another. What the heck, my curve ball had been hanging all day."

But it was that kind of year for Warren. His pitching

was superb, but the rest of the league had awakened to his talent and began throwing the best men on their staffs against him. Winning became tougher, and his team wasn't getting him runs. He lost one game to Brooklyn, 1–0, when a ground ball took a bad hop over the third baseman's head. But instead of moaning about his fate, Warren worried about the other fellow's feelings. In the clubhouse after that heartbreaking defeat, he said casually, but loudly enough for the errant third baseman Nanny Fernandez to hear, "Say, was I lucky they only got one run off me today. I was feeling terrible, didn't have my stuff today at all."

Midway through the season the Cardinals and Dodgers ran away from the rest of the league to fight between themselves for the pennant that Brooklyn eventually captured. But Spahn continued his brilliant way. In a game with the St. Louis Cardinals he unveiled his new slow curve, and it proved a potent weapon. It was a bases-loaded, two-out situation in a tight ball game. Warren got to two balls and two strikes on the batter, then motioned for catcher Phil Masi to come out to the mound.

Masi trotted out, mask under his arm. "What's the matter? You okay, Spahnnie?" he asked.

Warren nodded. "Sure. But I was just wondering. I was thinking this looked like a good spot to try that change-up curve I've been working on."

The catcher stared at him. "Here? Now? In a spot like this? You think it'll work?"

Spahn grinned. "We'll soon find out."

Masi grinned back, shrugged, then waddled back to

his position behind the plate. He squatted; Spahn, with the bases loaded, went into a full windup, kicked his right leg high and floated the slow curve up to the plate. The Cardinal batter, who had received four fast pitches in a row and was expecting nothing but more of the same, nearly broke his back as he swung out ahead of the tantalizing pitch for strike three.

With this new pitch in his repertoire, Warren continued to mow down the league. Maybe the Braves weren't hitting, but they didn't need very much to win behind Spahn. With his record at 17–10 in the last two weeks of the season, he stalked out to the mound determined to win twenty games, support or no support. And Warren did it, by pitching three straight shutouts and a 2–1 win in his last four games.

Third baseman Bob Elliott won the National League's Most Valuable Player award in 1947 for his part in bringing a third-place finish to the Braves. However, Spahn was easily the Braves' most valuable pitcher. His final record was 21–10, but in those ten losses the Braves scored a total of only eleven runs behind him, and were shut out five times!

Warren led the league in innings pitched, with two hundred ninety; in earned run average, 2.33; and in shutouts, with seven. He had been named to the National League's All-Star team, pitching two scoreless innings in the annual classic.

Particularly since he was virtually unknown in the major leagues, and certainly a question mark in talent when the season began, Spahn was the pitching sensation of 1947. Baseball writers polled a number of National Leaguers on the reasons for Warren's sudden success.

"He's got a great overhand curve," offered Ben Chapman, then manager of the Philadelphia Phillies.

"Terrific fast ball," said Pee Wee Reese of the Dodgers.

But it was his own receiver Phil Masi who said, "Control, that's Spahn's secret. That guy knows where every pitch is going."

In Buffalo, New York, reading Masi's comment in the newspaper, Ed Spahn thought back to the long hours spent in the back yard, practicing with his son. And he was able to smile with pride and satisfaction.

Chapter Seven ·

The Boston Braves of 1914 are inscribed in baseball history as the Miracle Team, because they climbed from last place in July, to win the pennant by ten and a half games. But to the citizens of Boston, the pennant-winning Braves of 1948 were equally miraculous. The new generation of baseball fans in Boston had come to accept the second division as the usual Braves' berth, and the possibility of a pennant flying over Braves Field never even entered their minds. Certainly, as the 1948 season began, the fans had little reason to expect anything like a pennant from the hodgepodge aggregation the Braves fielded.

Boston had two good pitchers, Warren Spahn and Johnny Sain. From their farm system the Braves brought up hurler Vern Bickford, with only a fair minor league record, and shortstop Al Dark, a hot-shot collegian with only one full year of pro ball experience. First baseman Earl Torgeson, promoted from the minors the year before, and veteran catcher Phil Masi were the only other two players who were strictly Boston products. Even right fielder Tommy Holmes, a Brave since 1942, was

Yankee minor league property until the Braves bought him. The bulk of the team was a collection of major league castoffs and waiver pick-ups.

Third baseman Bob Elliott had come from the Pittsburgh Pirates; second baseman Eddie Stanky from Brooklyn; first baseman Frank McCormick was from Philadelphia; utility infielder Connie Ryan from the Giants. In the outfield, Jeff Heath had been obtained from the American League's St. Louis Browns; Mike McCormick was from Cincinnati, and Jim Russell from Pittsburgh. Second-string catcher Bill Salkeld was likewise from Pittsburgh. Pitcher Red Barrett was obtained from the Cardinals, Bill Voiselle from the Giants, Nelson Potter from the American League's Philadelphia Athletics and Clyde Shoun from the Cincinnati Reds.

All in all, it was hardly a collection to inspire dreams of a pennant.

As the season unfolded, the Braves showed nothing to alter their followers' expectations. In June, holler guy Ed Stanky broke his ankle and was lost for most of the season. That same month, with a grandiose display of hoopla, the Braves signed a Rochester schoolboy pitcher named Johnny Antonelli, outbidding thirteen other clubs by giving the youngster a sixty-five thousand dollar bonus. Antonelli pitched a total of four innings that entire season. What's more, the extravagant bonus stirred no little resentment among some of the Braves veterans, a resentment that was to smolder and spread and finally contribute materially to the team's collapse the following year.

By June, too, it was painfully apparent that something was wrong with Spahn. The hop seemed to be gone from his fast ball, and the hitters were pasting him all around the league. Despite their understandable glee at being able to hit Warren's big pitch, many enemy batters, out of concern and respect for the well-liked Boston hurler, queried him about his ineffectiveness.

"Hey, Hooks, what happened to your fast ball?" was becoming a much asked question.

As was to be expected under such circumstances, Warren began receiving advice from dozens of people, from within baseball and without. Much of the advice was conflicting, amateurish and nonsensical. But when a pitcher loses his touch he is apt to lose his confidence as well; soon he begins to reach for advice like a drowning man grasping at straws.

Warren began experimenting. He tried altering his motion; he lengthened his stride toward home plate, then shortened it. He fooled with his delivery: first he tried holding the ball a fraction of a second longer before letting it loose, then he let it go a fraction of a second sooner. He tried gripping the ball differently; that didn't work, either. There was little else for Warren to do then but discard the fast ball as his major pitch. He went to the curve, particularly the slow overhand curve he had used successfully the year before, and the change-up. Both these pitches had been effective weapons for him; however, much of their success was due to the fact that Warren's blazing fast ball set up hitters to be unbalanced by a half-speed pitch. Now, no longer worried about having a fast ball blown right past them, enemy batters were able to step up and slam Warren's serves all over the ball park.

As if losing his fast ball wasn't enough to make his nights sleepless, in midseason Warren began worrying about his wife's physical condition. Lorene was expecting a baby and experiencing a rough time of it. The Spahns had taken an apartment in Brookline, a suburb of Boston, and whenever the Braves' road games were against an eastern team, Warren flew home between pitching assignments to be with his wife.

On the western swings, Warren sat fidgeting on the bench, his uneasy mind a thousand miles away. Often, in the middle of a game, he would bolt from the dugout, rush into the clubhouse and call home to assure himself that Lorene was all right. His pitching was so bad that he didn't even make the National League's All Star team that year.

Meanwhile, the Braves were having a three-way pennant fight with the Dodgers and Cardinals. Sain was pitching superbly and would wind up with twenty-four wins. Shortstop Al Dark, who was playing magnificently, was to receive the Rookie-of-the-Year award after the season. Except for Spahn, everybody on the team seemed to be having a better-than-average year, and on the occasions when the club showed signs of slipping, manager Southworth went into a line-up juggling act that eventually brought back a winning combination.

However, nobody in Boston was getting excited. The crowds at Braves Field were larger than they had been in many years, but this probably was as much due to the promotional work of the Braves' owners as the team's surprisingly successful play. Buying pitcher Antonelli for sixty-five thousand dollars was as much a publicity-inspired move as a strategic one. In addition, the Braves management had instituted giveaway days, when lucky ticket holders received valuable gifts. Television was introduced. In its infancy then, the magic screen served to publicize and promote the game of baseball; many years were to pass before television was to be blamed for killing attendance and chasing teams to new cities.

August 21st was a big day for Warren Spahn and a big one for Boston. It was the day both came alive. The Braves were in Brooklyn for a double-header, leading the league and the Brooklyn Dodgers by one game. When the Dodgers beat Johnny Sain in the opener, they took the league lead by a few percentage points. With Spahn scheduled to pitch in the second game, the Braves found themselves teetering on the brink of disaster, and the chances were very good that they would take the long plunge, too.

As the second game began, one of the pessimistic Boston writers called out his gloomy prediction to the other baseball reporters in the Ebbets Field press box, "Well, I guess we've had it for this season. Spahnnie couldn't beat the Dodgers here on his good days, and he hasn't been having many good days this year."

Writer Herb Goren, covering the Dodgers for the now-defunct New York *Sun*, echoed the Boston man's sentiments. "Yeah, the Dodgers are hot now," he said, "and if they take this game, they'll be a mighty tough club to catch."

The Braves realized the crucial aspect of this game, too, and as Spahn walked slowly out to the mound to pitch the last half of the first inning, he knew what he was up against—the Dodgers had already beaten him twice that season. He scuffed at the dirt behind the pitcher's mound and waited for Dodger lead-off hitter Pee Wee Reese to step in.

If only my fast ball would come back, he thought wearily.

The Braves drew first blood off Brooklyn hurler Preacher Roe, but the Dodgers came right back to tie the score at 1–1. Then, in the fifth inning, the Brooklyn hitters began to catch up with Spahn's slow stuff; only a double play prevented a Dodger score. In the sixth, when successive singles and a walk with one out loaded the bases for the Dodgers, the Braves' relief hurler Nelson Potter got up to work in the bull pen. Spahn kicked at the mound, bore down and got the next hitter on a foul pop to catcher Phil Masi. Then the dangerous Jackie Robinson stepped into the batter's box.

Spahn took a deep breath and looked down to Masi for the sign. He stretched, checked the runner at third and broke off a sharp curve that Robinson took for a strike. Another curve was outside for ball one. Robinson took a change-up for ball two and a slow curve for the third ball. Spahn took the return throw from his catcher and looked keenly at the Dodger batter.

He's laying off, Warren thought, waiting for me to

come in with my fast ball so he can whack it. And I've got to come in with it, too. A walk now would force in a run.

Suddenly catcher Masi called time and trotted out to the mound. "Whatta you think, Spahnnie?" he said.

Warren knew what Masi meant by the question. Do we take the chance with a curve ball and hope you don't walk Robinson, or do we take the chance with your not-so-fast ball and hope he doesn't hit it out of the park.

Spahn came to a sudden decision. "We go with the fast ball, Phil," he said.

Masi started to speak, then stopped. Spahn knew what was on his catcher's lips, however. Understandably, he didn't have confidence in the pitcher's fast ball any more. "It's the only way, Phil," Spahn said, not very confident himself. "I know Robbie's laying for it, but maybe he'll be too eager and I can get it past him."

The catcher nodded. "Sure, Spahnnie, you can do it," he said. But he didn't sound as though he believed it.

Masi lumbered back behind home plate and squatted into position. Robinson, in his fidgety manner, waved his bat back and forth, wiggled in the box, wiped the palm of his right hand on his trousers and tugged at his cap, waiting for Spahn to pitch.

Warren kept him waiting too long in their duel of nerves and Robinson stepped out of the batter's box. Then he dug back in, and Spahn stepped up on the mound, reared back, kicked high and came down with everything he could muster on his fast ball. Robinson uncoiled like a steel spring; his bat flashed—but the ball sped past him and boomed loudly into Masi's mitt for strike two.

The Dodger star retreated from the box and looked out at the Boston pitcher with new respect in his eyes. Catcher Masi called time again and ran out to the mound. He plunked the ball into Spahn's glove and slapped the hurler encouragingly on the arm.

"Spahnnie," he said, his face grim, "you haven't thrown a ball that hard all year. You got another one like that up your sleeve?"

Warren nodded. "I don't know what I did all of a sudden, but whatever it was, I'm going to do it again."

It was three balls and two strikes on Robinson then, with two out and the bases loaded in the tied ball game. The stage was set again—Masi squatted behind the plate, Robinson set himself in the batter's box and Spahn stepped up on the mound. He went into a full windup, coiled, kicked his right leg high, stepped down and blazed another fast ball across the plate. Again Robinson's dangerous bat flashed, but again the ball sped by into Masi's mitt—for strike three! Robinson was out, the Dodgers were out—and Spahn was out of the inning without being scored upon.

That was Brooklyn's last threat of the day. The Braves scored a run in the seventh to lead, 2–1, and Spahn came back to mow down the Dodger hitters in the last three innings. As suddenly and inexplicably as his fast ball had disappeared early that season, so did it reappear that day in Brooklyn. It was alive those last three innings, and the

Dodgers broke their backs trying to get a piece of the blazing fast ball.

The Braves won the game, 2–1, and to this day that game stands as the last one Spahn ever won at Ebbets Field. Unless some other National League team moves into the Brooklyn park someday, the record will so remain, too. Moreover, of the many victories in Spahn's book, few were more important than the one against the Dodgers that August day in 1948. It put the Braves back in the league lead and made them feel for the first time that season that the pennant could indeed be won.

In the Boston clubhouse later, the players could feel the new expectancy, the hope, the determination in the air. The Boston writers felt it, too, and the electric atmosphere was carried back to Boston in their stories. If Spahn is all right again, so the feeling went, who can stop us?

As the players dressed and chatted with the reporters, manager Billy Southworth stepped into the locker room and voiced what all were thinking. "Spahnnie really had it out there today," the Boston skipper said. He draped his arm around Warren's naked shoulders and surveyed the room. "We're gonna go all the way now—right, fellas?"

"Right, Skip."

"You bet, Skip."

"Nobody'll pass us now."

Southworth nodded his head in satisfaction as the players voiced their determination to win the pennant. Then he turned to the baseball writers. "From now on," he announced, "I'm going to pitch Spahn and Sain as often as their arms will allow. They'll pitch in rotation every other game if they can do it. We've got some open dates coming up in September, then it's going to be Spahn, Sain, then Spahn again right after the day off."

The pressure was on. All over. The Spahns' child had been expected around the end of August, but the days went into September and still there was no sign. Warren was becoming frantic. At one point his nervousness became so acute that one of his teammates remarked, "Say, who's having this baby, Spahnnie or his wife?"

The Dodgers and Cardinals remained relentlessly on Boston's trail. On Labor Day, September 6th, the Dodgers moved into Braves Field for a double-header. Brooklyn, two games behind, was grimly determined to sweep both games and gain the league lead.

Once again, it was Spahn against Preacher Roe in a bitter mound duel. Both aces were at their marvelous best, and at the end of nine innings the score was tied, 1–1. The game went into extra innings. Jackie Robinson led off the Dodger's half of the tenth inning by drawing a walk. Spahn watched the speedy Dodger infielder carefully. This was a strategic spot for Jackie to try for a steal of second.

Robinson edged off first, eying Spahn, checking back at first baseman Specs Torgeson who was holding the bag against him. Spahn stretched, came down to his stop position, kicked out with his right leg and threw—to first base! Too late, Robinson realized he had been caught flat footed by the pitcher's great deceptive motion. In desperation he plunged head first for the bag, but Spahn's throw nailed him easily.

As the umpire's thumb went up in the air with the "out" sign, the crowd roared its appreciation at Warren's neat pick-off play. Robinson picked himself up, disgustedly smacked the dirt out of his uniform and stomped back to the Dodger dugout, shaking his head in wonder.

Through the tenth, the eleventh, the twelfth inning, the game continued. Neither pitcher displayed signs of weakening. In the thirteenth inning Robinson came up again, and promptly rapped a single, only the fifth hit off Spahn. Warily this time, the Dodger infielder took his lead off first. As Spahn pitched to the plate, Robinson bluffed a run at second; Spahn ignored him. On the next pitch Robinson again bluffed a steal, but Warren made no move to throw to first.

The count was one and one on the Dodger batter. Robinson led off first, watching Spahn's movements cagily. The Boston hurler eyed the runner calmly, stretched, stopped, then threw—now to first! And again he had Robinson picked off! The Boston fans were delirious, howling and applauding and stamping their feet in glee at Spahn's amazing display of skill. Jackie leaped up and stormed at the umpire, but he was more angry at himself than outraged at the decision. The arbiter turned his back on the arguing player, and Robinson walked away gloomily, kicking at the dirt all the way back to the dugout.

Spahn retired the Dodgers in order in the fourteenth, and the Braves finally broke through in their half of the inning to score and win the game, 2–1. The defeat just about broke the back of the Dodgers. Johnny Sain then shut them out in the second game, and Brooklyn never recovered from the double defeat, eventually winding up in third place, behind the runner-up St. Louis Cardinals.

Spahn and Sain having done their jobs, the schedule and the weather moved in to help the Braves in their drive toward the National League pennant. After the double-header on the sixth of September, there were two open days. The Braves left Boston for Philadelphia, but it rained on the ninth and tenth. On the eleventh of September, when the Braves played a day-night double-header with the Phillies, they were able once again to call on their two aces Spahn and Sain.

The situation gave rise to the legend of the Braves' three-man pitching staff—Spahn, Sain and the weather— a legend which has gone down in baseball history in a rhyming slogan that was caught up by baseball fans everywhere that September: "Spahn, Sain, then pray for rain."

Johnny Sain beat the Phillies the afternoon of the eleventh, 3–1, and Spahn came back in the nightcap to win again, 13–2. The next day Barrett and Bickford split another double-header with Philadelphia.

The moment the second game was over, Spahn sped from the ball park to the airport and jumped on the first plane bound for Boston. The baby still hadn't arrived, and Lorene had been confined by her doctor to the Boston Lying-In Hospital, where she could be under constant observation.

All the next afternoon, Spahn paced in front of the Braves' dugout while Sain was beating the Cubs. On the following day he beat Chicago himself, 5–2, but between each pitch he glanced inquiringly at the bench to see whether any word had come from the hospital.

On the eighteenth day of September, with only two days rest, Spahn, hollow-eyed from lack of sleep, trudged out to the mound in Boston and pitched a four-hit victory over the Pirates, winning it, 2–1. At this point, with only two victories needed to win the pennant, and Warren obviously on the verge of a breakdown, manager Southworth broke the feverish pace of the pitching routine.

When Vern Bickford hurled the pennant clincher on September 26th, Warren wasn't even at the ball park to celebrate the victory; he was at the bedside of his wife. But he was still too early. Gregory Dee Spahn didn't arrive until October 1st.

Except for the final six weeks of the season, when "Spahn, Sain, then pray for rain" became the watchword in Boston, the 1948 campaign was one of Spahn's poorest. His record was 15–12, and only his spectacular clutch pitching in the stretch brought him above the .500 mark. Warren's earned-run average, 3.71, for a full season's pitching, stands as the worst of his career. Only in 1942, when he appeared in but four games for Boston and pitched sixteen innings, did he do worse—5.63.

With Boston's first pennant since 1914 in the bag on

September 26th, the Braves settled down to watch the finale of one of the hottest flag races in American League history. The day before the Braves' pennant clincher, there was still a three-way tie for first in the junior circuit, involving Cleveland, Boston and New York. The Indians opened up a two-game lead that looked insurmountable at that late stage of the race, but they dropped two of their last three games, the Red Sox swept their final three and the American League race ended in a tie.

Boston's enthusiastic citizens immediately saw visions of a local World Series, but it was strictly a mirage. In a one-game play-off, the Indians walloped the Red Sox, 8–3, in Boston's Fenway Park, then simply moved their equipment over to Braves Field for the oncoming series.

Chapter Eight ·

Compared with the motley crew that comprised the 1948 Braves, the Cleveland Indians of that year were a formidable team indeed. Boston's two front-line hurlers were Johnny Sain, who won twenty-four games that season, and Warren Spahn, with fifteen victories. Against these, Cleveland stacked two twenty-game winners, Bob Lemon and Gene Bearden, and the great Bob Feller, who had an "off" year, with nineteen victories.

The Indians had the best infield in baseball, too. Eddie Robinson was on first, former Yankee star Joe Gordon on second, Lou Boudreau, fielding brilliantly and hitting .355 for the season, was at shortstop and Ken Keltner was at third. In the outfield were Dale Mitchell, third best hitter in the league, plus Larry Doby and Allie Clark. Behind the plate was Jim Hegan. Cleveland's powerful pitching staff was further augmented by Steve Gromek, Sam Zoldak and the unbelievable Satchel Paige. The ageless Negro was officially listed as being forty-two years old then, but he was probably closer to fifty. Still, he won six and lost one for the Indians in 1948.

Manager Boudreau opened the series with Feller,

while Southworth selected Johnny Sain. It was Rapid Robert's first World Series appearance—and good enough to win almost any game. However, lack of hitting and a highly controversial umpire's decision cost him a 1–0 loss.

The Braves didn't get a hit off Feller until the fifth inning, when Marv Rickert singled. They didn't get their second—and last—hit until the eighth, but that one broke up the ball game. Catcher Bill Salkeld opened the Braves' eighth by drawing a walk. Phil Masi ran for Salkeld and was sacrificed to second by Mike McCormick. Boudreau then ordered an intentional walk to Eddie Stanky, bringing up pitcher Sain.

With the count one ball and one strike on Sain, shortstop Boudreau suddenly darted behind second base, took the quick pick-off throw from Feller, then slapped the ball on Masi. It was a close play and umpire Bill Stewart called Masi safe. Boudreau and the Indians stormed and fumed at Stewart, claiming that Masi had been tagged before he got back to the base. Photographs of the play seemed to show that Masi was, indeed, out. However, the angle from which a photograph is taken often distorts the actual situation, and Stewart's decision may have been correct.

At any rate, his decision certainly stood at the time. Masi was safe at second. Feller, who continued to throw warm-up pitches to his catcher while the argument raged, then retired Sain, but Tommy Holmes singled to score Masi with the game's only run. In the controversy over the decision at second base, Sain's pitching chore was almost overlooked; he had done superbly well himself, scattering four singles and not walking a man.

Spahn's introduction to World Series play next day was no happier than Feller's. Warren had no close decisions to blame, however; he was knocked out of the box cleanly. For the first three innings he set the Indians down easily with one hit, while his teammates got him a run in the first inning, for a 1–0 lead.

Then, in the fourth, Lou Boudreau cracked him for a double. Gordon singled to score the Cleveland manager with the tying run. Keltner advanced Gordon to second with a ground-out, and Larry Doby singled for the Indians' second run.

Dale Mitchell led off the Indians' fifth with a single. Allie Clark sacrificed and Kennedy walked. Then Warren bore down and got two quick strikes on Boudreau, but the Cleveland slugger rapped the next serve for a single, scoring Mitchell. That did it for Spahn. Southworth plodded out to the mound and called in Red Barrett from the bull pen. As Warren walked morosely off the mound to the dugout, catcher Salkeld called out to him, "Don't worry, Spahnnie, you'll get them next time."

He trudged into the dugout and sat down heavily on the bench. Johnny Sain walked over and sat down beside him. "A few inches the other way and a couple of those hits would have been outs," he said, commiserating with his friend. "You gave it a good try."

Warren smiled sourly. "A good try isn't enough for me, Johnny," he said. "I pitch to win them all, same as you."

Sain nodded understandingly, and the two pitchers

turned their attention back to the playing field. Spahn watched broodingly as relief pitcher Barrett put out the fire, too late to save the game, however.

What did I do wrong? Warren thought anxiously as he sat on the bench. Where did I slip up? he wondered. I seemed to have all my stuff. My fast ball was good, the curve was working. Maybe I was careless—the idea suddenly hit him. Maybe I wasn't getting the corners the way I should have. Maybe I wasn't pitching to their weak spots. He shook his head wearily and sighed. Maybe, maybe. Well, there's no maybe about the fact that the Indians belted me out of there, he told himself.

As Barrett got the third out to retire the Indians, Warren rose from the bench and walked down the steps to the clubhouse passageway. He heard Johnny Sain's voice call to him as he walked through the cool darkness of the corridor beneath the grandstand. "You'll beat 'em next time, Spahnnie."

Warren pressed his lips together grimly. You bet I'll beat them next time, he promised savagely. Then he strode into the Braves' locker room and stripped for his shower.

There almost wasn't any next time, however. The wizardry of the masterful Cleveland pitching staff continued as the scene shifted to the Indians's home grounds at Municipal Stadium. Gene Bearden shut out the Braves in the third game of the series, 2–0, beating Vern Bickford; and when Steve Gromek out-dueled Johnny Sain the next day, 2–1, the National League picture looked black.

Manager Billy Southworth was really up a tree for the fifth game. He was behind three games to one. The Indians needed one more game to win the series, and there were few optimists in baseball who gave the Braves much of a chance to stop them. Boston's weak hitting had accounted for only three runs in the first four games. Now Bob Feller was back, with three full days of rest behind him, to pitch against them. And whom did Southworth have to throw against Feller? Sain had pitched the day before, and Spahn had had only two days rest. Besides, he hadn't looked sharp against Cleveland his first time against them. Out of sheer desperation, Southworth went to Nelson Potter.

The largest crowd in World Series history, 86,288, overflowed Municipal Stadium on October 10th to be in on Cleveland's clincher. The disillusionment was quick, however. Tommy Holmes opened against Feller with a single. Dark singled, Torgeson flied out, but Bob Elliott slammed a three-run home run into the right field stands.

Cleveland got one run back for Feller in its half of the first inning on a lead-off home run by Dale Mitchell, but Elliott hit his second homer in succession in the third, making the score 4–1 in favor of Boston.

The roof fell in on Potter in the fourth inning. Joe Gordon opened with a single. When Keltner drew a walk, manager Southworth signaled to his bull pen; Spahn and Barrett began warming up. Judnich singled, scoring Gordon, and closing the score to 4–2. Southworth called time and walked slowly out to the mound. His mission for the moment was a time-wasting one; he wanted to give the embattled Potter a breather, and at the same time afford his bull pen hurlers more time to warm up.

"How you feeling, Nels?" he asked Potter.

The pitcher shrugged, "I still have my stuff."

Catcher Salkeld joined them at the mound. Southworth turned to him. "Whatta you say, Bill? He still got it?"

"The curve's been hanging a little, but I think we can last this one out. Let's give the bull pen a little more time, anyway."

Finally Southworth and Salkeld returned and Potter went back to work. He got Eddie Robinson out, but it was on a hard line drive to shortstop Dark. Southworth looked anxiously out at his bull pen, hesitated, then let Potter go on. But the Braves hurler didn't have his stuff. Jim Hegan cracked his first pitch for a home run into the left field stands.

The huge crowd of Cleveland partisans went wild. The Indians held the lead now, 5–4, and the World's Championship was just minutes away. As Hegan trotted around the bases, Southworth rose wearily from the bench and walked out to the mound. He stood there a moment with catcher Salkeld and the dejected Potter, squinting out at the bullpen, making up his mind. Umpire Babe Pinelli came over to them. "Well, what'll it be, Billy?" he asked Southworth.

The Braves pilot sighed, shrugged and waved his left hand, indicating that he wanted his left-hander to come in to relieve Potter. He wanted Warren Spahn.

Warren strode deliberately in from the bull pen, his face set and grim. After his failure in the second game of the series, he wanted very badly to pull this one out of the fire. He wanted it for himself, for the Braves and for Lorene, who, he knew, was watching the game on television from her hospital bed in Boston.

He took the ball from Southworth, muttered a few words of commiseration to Potter, then nodded to catcher Salkeld. "Let's hold 'em, Bill," he said. "Nobody hits from now on."

Salkeld tapped him encouragingly with his mitt. "Just fog 'em in there, Spahnnie, these guys can't hit."

The catcher trotted back behind the plate; Spahn took his last few warm-up tosses and indicated that he was ready. Bob Feller stepped in to hit for Cleveland. Warren wound up, threw—and blazed three fast balls right past the Cleveland hurler to strike him out. Dale Mitchell then popped out, to end the Indians' rally. They led now, 5–4, however.

Spahn set the Indians down without any trouble in the fifth inning, and in the sixth Salkeld homered to tie the game, 5–5. Warren was now responsible for the decision, and he set to work with renewed determination.

He retired Cleveland in order again in the sixth. Then, in the seventh, the Braves broke through and knocked Feller out of the box. Holmes started the rally with a single. Dark sacrificed him to second. Torgeson singled, for the tie-breaking run. Feller was taken out and Ed Klieman came in to pitch.

Klieman didn't get a man out and Russ Christopher

was called upon to check the Braves' attack. But the Boston team was aroused now, fighting with its back to the wall. Christopher, greeted with successive singles by McCormick and Stanky, was immediately relieved by Satchel Paige, who promptly walked Spahn with the bases loaded, forcing in the fifth Braves' run of the inning. A sixth run was added before Paige could put out the fire, and Boston took over an 11–5 lead.

Spahn breezed through the seventh, still not giving up a hit. But Lou Boudreau opened the eighth with a booming double. Catcher Salkeld called for time and trotted out to the mound. "You getting tired, Spahnnie?"

Warren shook his head. "I feel great. Boudreau got lucky."

Salkeld nodded. "Okay, kid, let's get the rest of these guys now. Wrap this one up for us, Spahnnie."

Warren grinned. "In a blue ribbon, Bill. Watch out for your hand. From now on I'm going to show these guys what a fast ball really looks like."

Salkeld walked back behind the plate and squatted to give the sign. Warren stretched, checked Boudreau, then threw to the dangerous Joe Gordon. The Cleveland second baseman swung and missed at a fast ball. Spahn came back with a big curve. Gordon swung and missed again—strike two. Warren wasted a pitch on the outside, then threw a fast ball. Gordon swung and missed. Strike three; Salkeld came out from behind the plate and shook his fist encouragingly at the mound.

"Atta boy, Spahnnie," he called. "That's burning 'em in there, Spahnnie boy!"

Ken Keltner stepped into the batter's box. Both dugouts were alive with chatter now, the Indians calling for a rally, the Braves calling on Spahn to keep the enemy in check. "Get a hold of one, Kenny," came the cry from the Cleveland bench. "No hitter in there, Spahnnie!" shouted the Boston players.

Warren scowled down at the batter. He stretched, looked back at Boudreau, turned, kicked high and buzzed a fast ball down the middle for a strike. Keltner stepped out of the box, rubbed dirt on his hands, stepped back in. Spahn stretched, kicked and threw. Ball one. He stretched, kicked and threw again. Keltner swung and missed at a sharp curve. Strike two. Warren shook off Salkeld's sign for a curve, came back with his fast ball. Keltner swung and missed. Strike three!

Ray Boone came in to pinch-hit for Walt Judnich. Spahn was working like a machine now, his arms and legs churning and jerking like pistons. A stretch, a kick and a throw—and fast balls shot from his left arm like bullets from a rifle. Boone never had a chance; nobody would have had—the way Spahn was going that afternoon. The Cleveland hitter swung vainly at three fast balls he barely saw. Warren had struck out the side!

In the ninth he continued his mastery. He got Eddie Robinson on a pop-up. Then up stepped Jim Hegan, whose homer earlier in the game had given Cleveland its brief lead. Spahn threw a fast ball right by Hegan, then snapped off two vicious curve balls that made the Cleveland catcher look foolish as he lunged futiley at the ball. Two out—one to go for Warren's first World Series win.

Though six runs behind, the Indians played it out to the end. There were too many examples in baseball history to let them forget that the game isn't over until the last out is recorded. Cleveland's Eric Tipton came in to pinch-hit for relief pitcher Bob Muncrief.

But Spahn wasn't going to let this game get away. Tipton couldn't even touch him for a foul. Three times that right leg of Warren's kicked high in the air, three times the left arm flashed downward. And three times a white blur flew past Tipton's bat. Another strike-out. Three out —and the ball game was over!

Warren's teammates mobbed him as he walked off the mound. They rushed him from the outfield and the infield and they poured out of the dugout to surround him, pump his hand and pat him on the back. Even the partisan Cleveland crowd, who had come to see their Indians crowned champions that day, stood up and applauded one of the finest pieces of clutch pitching ever seen in a World Series.

In winning his first World Series game, keeping the Braves' hopes alive for eventual victory, Warren pitched five and two-thirds innings, allowed but one hit and walked one man. He struck out seven of the nineteen men who faced him, including five of the last six.

It was quite a hurling performance, and though, as it turned out, that was the Braves' last gasp of the series, Warren had an opportunity to display more of the same the following day.

Pitching depth told the story in the final game, for while Boston's Billy Southworth had to dig into the barrel for Bill Voiselle, a relief pitcher who had seen action in the third game, Cleveland was able to start twenty-game winner Bob Lemon, who had beaten the Braves in the second game. At that, Voiselle acquitted himself creditably, and except for a couple of bad breaks, the verdict might have gone the other way.

The Indians tallied first, on doubles by Mitchell and Boudreau in the third inning. The Braves came back with a run in the fourth, and had Southworth been able to count on a rested relief pitcher that early in the game, the Braves might have scored more. As it turned out, with bases loaded, two out and pitcher Voiselle at bat, Southworth took a look at what was available in the bull pen and let Voiselle hit for himself. The pitcher grounded out to choke off the potential of a big inning.

However, when the Indians scored twice more in the sixth, Southworth was forced to make a move. He knew he had to pinch-hit for Voiselle at the pitcher's next turn at bat, and to keep the Indians within range, he needed the best pitcher available. The Boston pilot walked to the end of the bench and sat down next to Spahn. He said nothing for a moment, staring out at the field. He knew the effort Warren had put into his brilliant relief turn the day before. But the chips were down here. If the Braves lost this game, the man would have all winter to rest.

"Think you can go in there?" he asked abruptly.

Warren didn't hesitate. "I'll give it all I've got," he said simply.

Southworth nodded. "I know." He patted the pitcher's knee. "Okay, warm up. Voiselle will probably be coming up to hit in the seventh. We'll pinch-hit for him and you'll go in the eighth."

Spahn removed his warm-up jacket and trotted out to the bull pen. His arm felt a little stiff from the previous day's work, and when he strode out to pitch the eighth, with the score 3–1 Cleveland, it was still feeling stiff. The first batter he faced was Joe Gordon, and Warren knew his pitching was off when Gordon smacked a whistling line drive to left center that Marv Rickert just did catch.

But Keltner, Thurman Tucker and Robinson rapped him quickly for successive singles to make the score 4–1. Southworth bobbed out of the dugout and hurried to the mound. Spahn stood there calmly. "I'm okay," he said to his skipper. "I couldn't get loose, but I think I worked it out now."

Tucker was on third, Robinson was on first and catcher Hegan was at bat. Warren stretched, checked the runners and threw a strike past Hegan. He took the return toss from Salkeld, stretched, kicked and threw—but to first! And Robinson was picked off! Warren's move was so deceptive, the runner didn't even have a chance to slide. With two out now, Spahn went back to work on Hegan. He slipped a second strike past the Cleveland catcher. A curve was outside for ball one. Hegan fouled off the next pitch, then broke his back flailing desperately at a curve that broke away from him for strike three.

Enlivened by Spahn's spectacular pick-off play and strike-out of Hegan, the Braves stormed back with two runs in their half of the eighth. Holmes singled, and after Dark went out, Torgeson, who led Boston's series hitting with .389, came up with a double. Elliott walked to load the bases, and Cleveland pitcher Lemon walked to the showers, replaced on the mound by Gene Bearden. Clint Conatser, batting for Rickert, drove in a run with a fly ball to Tucker. Masi batted for Salkeld and doubled, narrowing the gap to 4–3. But Mike McCormick bounced out to end the rally.

Spahn went out to pitch the ninth, angry at himself and at the Indians. If he hadn't allowed the Cleveland run in the eighth, the Braves' two-run rally would have tied the score. "They won't even smell the ball this inning," he promised himself as he stalked to the mound.

Pitcher Gene Bearden was Cleveland's first batter. He stood with his bat on his shoulder while two fast balls blew by him for two strikes, then waved feebly at the third bullet. Bearden walked away from the plate, shaking his head. As he passed Bob Kennedy, the next batter, he remarked, "Don't stop to blink in there, or you'll never get to see the ball. That guy is fast today."

Kennedy quickly discovered that fact for himself. Spahn was the picture of pitching artistry as he worked. Smoothly, effortlessly, he wound up, threw his leg high and came down with fast balls and curves that hopped and dipped Kennedy into a helpless tangle at home plate.

Kennedy struck out on four pitches. Larry Doby did better. He struck out on five. For the second day in a row, Warren had gone through an inning by striking out the side. This time he had gotten four men straight, too.

However, his effort was in vain. Eddie Stanky gave the Boston fans a momentary thrill when he opened the Braves' ninth by drawing a walk, but Sibby Sisti, batting for Spahn, bunted into a double play. Holmes flied out— and the series was over. The Cleveland Indians were World Champions.

As the season had gone for the Braves, so had gone the World Series; Boston's two victories were recorded by Spahn and Sain, the two pitchers whose fantastic feats of endurance and skill in the last month of the season had brought Boston a pennant. Warren emerged from the series with a 1–1 record. In the twelve innings he pitched, he allowed four runs, ten hits, struck out twelve, walked three. But eleven of his twelve strike-outs were gained in his final two appearances, in relief, in seven and two-thirds innings of pitching.

Despite their loss to the Indians in the World Series, the Boston players, Spahn included, looked forward to significant salary increases during the winter negotiations. After all, they had brought Boston its first pennant since 1914. But many of the players were due to be disappointed; the Braves were on the verge of bitter dissension that was to crack them wide open the following season.

Chapter Nine ·

The locker room of the Boston Braves' spring training camp at Bradenton, Florida, was quiet; but it was an uneasy quiet, sullen and tense and ominous. A locker door clanged, spiked shoes clattered on concrete, a shower hissed in a stall. But there were no voices; the easy chatter and banter of the usual baseball team clubhouse was missing. The Boston players were dressing silently, hardly glancing at each other. Then pitcher Red Barrett slammed his locker door shut with a resounding bang and turned to face the room.

"Listen, you guys, I'm getting disgusted with all this!" he announced to no one in particular. "We're acting like a bunch of babies who had our candy taken away, instead of like big league ballplayers."

One of the players stopped toweling himself and walked over to the pitcher. "I had more than candy taken away, Red. I had bread and butter. Steak and potatoes."

"You didn't have anything taken away," Barrett denied. "You just got less than you figured on, that's all."

"Less than I deserved, you mean," the other came back. "And so did a dozen other guys in this room."

Murmured assents came from around the room. "Yeah, Red," one Braves veteran spoke up, "most of us got a raw deal and you know it. Heck, we win the first pennant seen in this town in almost thirty-five years—and what do we get for it? Peanuts!"

"And whose fault is it?" a new voice put in. "I'll tell you whose. Southworth's. He juggled the line-up so much we all looked like a bunch of bush leaguers trying to make the team, while he grabbed the credit for being a mastermind."

"That's right," still another player said. "When I asked for more money they said to me, 'Well, you were out of a lot of games last year. We don't know that you're worth that much money to us.'"

"Me, too."

"Yeah, that's what they told me."

The rebellious voices rose in chorus, expressing the resentment of the Braves at what they felt were insufficient raises in salary for the coming 1949 season. Considering that they had won the pennant, the players expected substantial increases. When they were not forthcoming, many of them blamed manager Southworth, claiming he sided with the Braves' front office, instead of with them. Also, as several of the players voiced in the locker room, they considered that in maneuvering his line-ups throughout the season, he minimized the importance of the players in their fight for the pennant.

However, the seeds of the dissension had been sown during the previous season. Southworth was a strict disciplinarian, and many players chafed under his tight rein.

He was formal, distant, often nervous and inconsistent, characteristics which nettled some of the writers covering the club, in addition to the players. Many times the Boston manager announced a pitching rotation, or a change in line-up, and then did something entirely different. To baseball writers, this is annoying, because it can make them appear inaccurate to the reading public. However, to the men on the team, it is a morale destroyer, tending to injure their self-confidence and their confidence in the ability of their manager.

In the common fight for the pennant in 1948, the Braves had submerged their dissatisfaction, but when the salary disputes began with the Braves' front office that winter, the wounds reopened; by spring they were raw and ugly.

In the locker room in Bradenton, pitcher Red Barrett continued his attempt to tie the team together.

"Okay, okay, I admit some of you guys have gripes. I'm with you. Don't anyone think I'm stooging for the front office. But I'm being practical. What's the good of all this moping around and everybody trying to knife everybody else in the back? Where's that going to get us? The way you guys looked on the field today you couldn't make the first division in the Boy Scouts league."

"You got a suggestion to make, Red?" someone called. "Maybe we should send a note of thanks to the front office and Southworth, thanking them for cutting our throats?"

"Yes, I've got a suggestion to make," Barrett countered. "I suggest we forget about what's done and can't be helped—and go out and win another pennant. I didn't hear anyone complain last year about getting that extra forty-five hundred dollars from the World Series."

The pitcher's suggestion at a truce was met with silence. "Listen," he persisted, "this thing has been getting us bad publicity. The papers are after us and after Southworth. Even if you don't feel that way now, I think it would be a good idea for us to give Billy our vote of confidence, just to quiet this down, if nothing else."

Players began shaking their heads. "Not me." "Count me out."

"I wouldn't vote Southworth for dog catcher," one player growled. "Look, who's a more easygoing guy than Spahnnie?" the man continued, "and where's he today? He isn't even here. He's so sore at what they offered him he hasn't even signed his contract yet."

"That's right," another chimed in. "Is there a fairer-minded guy in this room than ol' Hooks? If he was here today and said we should go along with Southworth, well, maybe I'd do it. But I heard that he said he'd rather play for a second division club than for Southworth."

"Spahnnie wouldn't ever say a thing like that, even if he thought it," someone said sharply.

"Well, maybe he said it and maybe he didn't," the first player conceded. (Warren later denied he made the statement.) "But he's not signed yet, and that means enough to us."

Pitcher Barrett lost his fight to calm the troubled waters; the Braves refused to announce a vote of confidence for manager Southworth; the feud was still on.

Meanwhile, back at his ranch Spahn awaited further word from the Braves about his salary for 1949. The Spahns had purchased their ranch the year before, in Hartshorne, Oklahoma, where Lorene's parents lived. After a youth spent in the city, Warren found that he preferred ranch life, especially as a change from the hectic days of the baseball season. But just to keep him from getting too homesick for his profession, Spahn's ranch neighbor was Pepper Martin, the great third baseman and outfielder of the old St. Louis Cardinals' Gas House Gang.

Warren's salary dispute with the Braves began in January, when the Boston management mailed his 1949 contract. His normally unshakable calm came close to breaking when he saw what the Braves had offered. Angrily, he mailed back the contract—unsigned.

The duel between them was still raging when spring training began in February. General manager John Quinn phoned him.

"You come down a little, we'll go up a little," he offered. "We've always treated you right, Warren."

"I'll come down a little," Spahn agreed, "but you'll have to come up a lot. My record deserves better."

"You were fifteen and twelve," Quinn stated the fact simply.

"But remember September," Warren countered. "I won them when we needed them most. Sain and me. Remember?"

Thus the disagreement continued, neither man willing to concede too much, yet both anxious to get the matter settled. Quinn was concerned about the obvious dissension tearing at the team, and he knew that Spahn's holdout wasn't helping. At the same time, while determined to get at least approximately what he asked for, Warren was eager to get to spring training in time to work himself into shape for opening day.

Finally, on March 5th, the Braves announced that Spahn had agreed to terms and was leaving for Bradenton at once. Manager Southworth immediately predicted that Warren would win twenty games that season.

"He's one of the best left-handers in the league, if not the best," enthused Southworth to reporters. "It may have been my fault that Spahn didn't repeat his 1947 success last season. It may be that I neglected him too much, took too much for granted. But I can promise that this year he will be checked thoroughly."

The Boston manager predicted accurately Spahn's successful year, but he wasn't around to see it come to pass. As the season opened and progressed through spring, it became increasingly apparent that Southworth couldn't control the antagonistic faction on the Braves. Tighter discipline resulted only in more flagrant and arrogant breaches of his rules. The team floundered in the second division. Dissension wasn't the only thing hounding the club; pitcher Johnny Sain developed arm trouble, shortstop Al Dark was suffering from the "sophomore jinx," his play falling far below his rookie-of-the-year form of 1948, and Earl Torgeson was side-lined with a separated shoulder and broken thumb.

Serenely, through the storm and the mutiny, sailed the

tall, lean form of Warren Spahn. Calmly, stolidly, when his turn came to pitch he took his place on the mound in front of a disorganized, dispirited team and hurled victory after victory. Time after time, when it seemed imminent that the Braves would fall through the bottom of the league, Spahn came up with a big game to stop a losing streak.

But he couldn't carry the Braves alone. In August, manager Southworth appeared to be heading for a breakdown, due to the strain of piloting a losing and rebellious team. Although for his own good, Braves president Lou Perini could no longer retain him, he backed Southworth in the dispute. On August 16th, Perini announced that for reasons of ill health Southworth was being relieved of his duties as manager of the Boston Braves.

"But," Perini added, "he will be back in 1950."

The baseball writers were skeptical. "If Southworth comes back in 1950," one of them wrote, "it's a sure bet a lot of the players won't."

Coach Johnny Cooney finished the season as acting manager. "I don't like this job," he told the Boston players when he took over, "and I didn't ask for it. But we're all stuck with it, so let's see if we can't go out and play a little baseball for a change."

With the abrasive handling of manager Southworth no longer a deterrent, the Braves tried to right themselves. But the fact was—Southworth or no—they didn't have it that year. Soon after Cooney took over the helm, they dropped seven straight before a heroic 1–0 victory by Spahn over the Phillies halted the slide.

In the closing days of the season, fourth place—the bottom rung of the first division—was a battle between the Giants and the faltering Braves. Twice, in the final stages, the Giants came within one game of catching Boston; each time Spahn came in to send the Giants tumbling downward. When the season ended, just two games separated the fourth-place Braves and the fifth-place New Yorkers.

Considering the handicap Warren pitched under with the discordant crew of 1948 Braves, baseball experts regard his record for the year as one of the most remarkable pitching feats in baseball annals. He led the league in wins, with twenty-one against fourteen losses; he led in strike-outs, with one hundred fifty-one, total innings pitched, three hundred two, and games completed, twenty-five.

As Braves president Lou Perini promised, Billy Southworth was rehired for the 1950 season. And as the experts predicted, many of the 1949 Braves did not come back. Thirteen players from that team were traded off, sold or sent down to the minors, including the shortstop–second base combination of Al Dark and Eddie Stanky. During the winter, these two were traded to the Giants for outfielders Willard Marshall, Sid Gordon, shortstop Buddy Kerr and pitcher Sam Webb.

Spahn appeared pleased with the deal. "Both Gordon and Marshall were rough hitters for me," he told Jerry Mitchell of the New York *Post*. "And they're good outfielders, too. I'm a fast-ball pitcher, and that means most of the balls hit off me go up in the air, to the outfield, so I appreciate good outfielding."

Despite the wholesale transfusion of new blood and the maneuverings of a regenerated, more liberal-minded Southworth, the Braves could not improve on their previous year's fourth-place finish. Except for speedy outfielder Sam Jethroe, Boston's first Negro player, they were old and slow, and it was generally conceded that Southworth did well by wheedling them into fourth place.

For the second straight year Spahn won twenty-one games, best in the league, but he lost seventeen. Again, too, he was top man in the strike-out department, with one hundred ninety-one.

Peculiarly, it wasn't until after the worst season of his career that Warren began to receive the accolades long due him. Perhaps it was his sudden inability to win that prompted fans and experts to wake up to the fact that he had been one of baseball's winningest pitchers for several years, without anybody noticing it.

At any rate, after posting a 22–14 record with the again fourth-place Braves in 1951, and tying the Dodgers' Don Newcombe for the strike-out lead with one hundred sixty-four, Spahn ran into an incredible streak of bad luck and bad support in 1952. The misfortune and misplays Warren suffered that year would have driven a less patient pitcher out of his mind. He endured the first and only losing season of his baseball life, winning fourteen while dropping nineteen. It might easily have been the other way around—and then some. Indicative of the

kind of hard luck year Spahn had were his other pitching statistics: he was still the strike-out leader, with one
hundred eighty-three, he had the eleventh best earned
average in the league, with 2.98, and was third in the
league in completed games, with nineteen. Six of his
losses were by one run; the Braves, who finished seventh
that dismal year, were exceeded in losing one-run decisions only by the last-place Pittsburgh Pirates.

There were times that season when Warren's bad luck
had to be seen to be believed. There was the game
against the Cubs on June 14th, for example. He faced the
knuckle ball artist Willard Ramsdell that day, and for
five innings both men pitched scoreless ball. After a first
inning triple to George Crowe, Ramsdell hadn't allowed
another hit throughout those five frames. Then, in the
sixth, Spahn took hitting matters into his own hands. He
picked out a knuckle ball and socked it into the Cubs'
bull pen in right field for a home run.

Ramsdell did better with the other Braves. After Warren's home run, he again held them hitless until lifted for
a pinch hitter in the eighth. Spahn continued to nurse
his self-made 1–0 lead, retaining it until the ninth. Then
Bill Serena whacked a home run over the left field fence
to tie the score. Johnny Klippstein, the Cubs' relief
pitcher, set Boston's hitless wonders down in order in the
home half of the ninth, and the game went into extra
innings.

Perhaps remembering a painful 2–1 loss in sixteen innings to the Dodgers the year before, Spahn came out
to pitch the tenth determined to shut out the Cubs the

rest of the day and night if necessary; he was getting tired of losing extra-inning ball games. He began throwing bullets to the Cub hitters, who, from the tenth inning on, hit nothing but the air in Braves Field.

But the Cubs had a fresh hurler going for them in Klippstein, and a pitcher didn't have to throw bullets against the 1952 Braves to get them out. Johnny Logan singled for Boston's third hit in the tenth inning, and catcher Ebba St. Claire singled in the fifteenth.

Meanwhile, Warren had the Cubs muttering to themselves as they tried to hit his fast ball. As the game went into the fifteenth inning, he had racked up seventeen strike-outs; thirteen Cubs had gone down swinging, four had looked at the third strike. Also, Spahn had not walked a man up to that point.

With one out in the fifteenth, he gave up his first pass—to Roy Smalley. Klippstein sacrificed Roy to second and Eddie Miksis was walked intentionally, in order to set up a double-play situation on the base paths. Up stepped Hal Jeffcoat. Spahn's first pitch was a curve outside for a ball. Visibly tiring now, he came back with a fast ball that was low, making it ball two. He threw another fast ball and Jeffcoat pounced on it. At the hard, clean, crack of the bat, Warren's shoulders sagged; he knew the ball was tagged hard.

In center field, Sam Jethroe turned and raced straight back, but even that fleet-footed outfielder couldn't catch up with the ball. It sailed over his head and ricocheted off the wall in left center field. By the time the ball was thrown back to the infield, Jeffcoat was at third with a triple—and two runs were across the plate. Spahn retired Serena on a pop-up and struck out Hank Sauer, but the damage was done. He lost the game, 3–1.

Until baseball writer Ed Costello of the Boston *Herald* informed him in the clubhouse later, Warren was unaware that he had struck out eighteen men to set a National League record and tie a major league one.

"Bob Feller got his eighteen in a nine inning game," Costello told Spahn. "But it's still tops for a game of any length. Dizzy Dean struck out seventeen in a nine-inning game, but nobody in the National League ever got more than that at any time until you did it today."

"Great," Spahn said dejectedly, "but I lost the game."

Costello clucked his tongue in sympathy. "You got some tough breaks today, Warren. It was a hard one to lose."

A pitcher losing a game under such circumstances would hardly be blamed for readily accepting the "out" offered by the reporter's comment about the bad breaks. But Warren's comment was typical of his honesty and unassuming attitude that has earned him unreserved respect around the league.

"Imagine me throwing a home run ball like that in the ninth inning and then walking Smalley. I deserved to lose that one," he said to Costello.

Deserving or not, it was that kind of year for him. Four days after dropping that marathon, he lost another 3–1 decision, this time to the Reds, in which he struck out eleven men in the regulation nine innings. That made it twenty-nine strike-outs in two successive games, breaking the major league record of twenty eight set by Feller in 1938. But while Bob won his two games, Spahn lost his two. Although Boston got seven hits against the Reds, they could score only one lone run—Sid Gordon's homer.

In the twenty-four innings pitched by Warren while setting his strike-out record, his teammates had supported him with a grand total of eleven hits and two runs. And one of those tallies was accounted for by his own home run.

"It looks as though Spahn is going to have to pitch nothing but shutouts to win a ball game," a baseball writer commented after the two straight 3–1 losses. "And with his luck, they'll become nothing-nothing ties!"

The man's jest turned out to be a fairly accurate prediction. Of Warren's fourteen victories in 1952, five were shutouts.

In the paradox of his fine pitching but poor won-lost record that year, many baseball people began to see Spahn for the first time as one of the great hurlers of the game. Quietly, without publicity-drawing flamboyancy or histrionics, he emerged at the end of the 1952 season as the outstanding pitcher in the National League. Statistics revealed that since joining the Braves in 1942, he won one hundred twenty-two games, more than any other active pitcher in the league; he pitched the most complete games, one hundred forty-two; he was the strike-out king, with an even one thousand. Spahn's earned-run average was surpassed then only by Max Lanier's of the Cardinals and Sal Maglie's of the Giants, and his shutout total of twenty-seven was second only to Boots Raffensberger's thirty.

That Spahn's talents until that point had gone virtually unheralded was not particularly surprising, considering his modest personality.

"If only he would pop off at something," sports writer Al Hirshberg remarked. "If he'd pick a fight with an umpire, threaten to bean a batter, insult a newspaperman—or do anything like that—he'd be more readily recognized. But Spahn is a pitcher, not a color artist."

However, it might be noted that color was not lacking entirely in that dismal edition of the 1952 Braves. In May the Braves fired manager Tommy Holmes, who had replaced Billy Southworth the year before, and gave the job to Charley Grimm. Easygoing, informal, likable, "Jolly Cholly" had the reputation of being one of the funniest men in baseball, and one of the greatest managers. When the Braves called on him, Grimm was managing their farm team in Milwaukee, the Brewers, with whom he had won the 1951 American Association pennant.

Grimm needed to watch his new charges in but one game to realize what he had inherited. But he took the blow with characteristic good humor. "I'm keeping my bags packed," he cracked to a Boston writer. "I don't know how long this will last, but I got a hunch I'm going to be back in Milwaukee before very long."

How accurate a prophet he was, Grimm could not know, of course. He was headed back for Milwaukee indeed, but not to pilot the Milwaukee Brewers again.

Behind the scenes, baseball magnates were staring at the red ink in their ledgers and seeking a solution to their financial problems. Wheels were beginning to turn.

The miracle of the Milwaukee Braves was just around the corner.

Chapter Ten ·

The machinations, transactions, negotiations and maneuverings which culminated in the shifting of the Braves' franchise from Boston to Milwaukee in the spring of 1953 could fill a book. To the general public the transfer appeared quite sudden, particularly since it was not approved and announced until the middle of March, less than a month before opening day. The Braves had been contemplating the shift for some time, however; they had lost more than a million dollars during the previous three years, and owner Lou Perini was eying Milwaukee, where the Braves owned the American Association's Brewers club, as a possible remedy for the annual plague of red ink.

It is quite likely that Perini had intended to wait until 1954 before moving, but his hand was forced in the spring of 1953; hence the suddenness of the announcement. What prompted Perini was the attempt by Bill Veeck, then owner of the St. Louis Browns, to move his team to Milwaukee. Blocked by Perini, the Browns eventually shifted to Baltimore and became the Orioles.

Perini's maneuverings against the Browns, by refusing

to move his Brewers team from Milwaukee, stirred no little resentment among the citizens of the Wisconsin city. They wanted a major league ball club, and Perini was denying them one. The Milwaukee sports writers took up the general cry against him.

The Braves' owner was on the hook. Since he intended to move to Milwaukee eventually, it would be poor policy to alienate the press and the public there. At the Braves' training camp in Florida, Perini pondered the problem. Finally, he called a press conference for the morning of March 14th, at the Bradenton ball park where the Braves trained.

Perini strode briskly into the pressroom that morning, nodded to the assembled sports writers and got right to the point. "Gentlemen," he announced, "I'm going to ask the National League for permission to open the season in Milwaukee."

The news was greeted by the Braves players with general enthusiasm; it hadn't been much fun playing before the meager, apathetic crowds in Braves Field. Spahn was one of the few who felt a pang of regret at leaving Boston.

"I broke into the majors in Boston," Warren explained, "and Lorene and I had an apartment up there which we used during the season. I guess I have kind of a sentimental attachment for the place."

He actually had more than just a sentimental attachment for Boston, but it wasn't like Spahn to mention it to anybody. With his friend Joel Greenberg, he had just invested a substantial amount of money in a diner—right across the street from Braves Field. With the team moving, Warren stood a good chance of losing twenty-five thousand dollars. But he didn't explain. When the diner was mentioned to him, he simply smiled a little wryly.

"Well, at least I won't have to spend my spare time there," he said.

Fortunately, the diner turned out to be a tremendous success, even without the patronage from Braves Field.

The manner in which the Milwaukee citizens greeted and treated their newly adopted sons is history. Dodger fans—the Brooklyn version, that is—were supposed to be the most fiercely partisan and passionate in baseball, but they were stonyhearted ingrates compared with the hysterical followers of the Milwaukee Braves.

The city's new ball park, County Stadium, was practically sold out of reserved seats for the season by the time opening day arrived in Milwaukee—one day late. The Braves' opener was in Cincinnati, and when they beat the Redlegs 2–0, it further served to whet the appetite of the impatient Milwaukee fans. The Braves were greeted in their new home the next day like conquering heroes, like pennant winners, instead of a team that had simply won its first game of the season.

County Stadium was bedlam for the historical contest of April 14th. The park was jammed to the rafters long before game time, and when the Braves began pouring onto the field from the clubhouse for batting practice, a thunderous roar burst from the crowd.

The Braves looked around at the solidly packed grandstands in genuine awe.

"Wow!" blurted third baseman Sibby Sisti, "I don't think we drew this many people all year in Boston!"

Outfielder Andy Pafko, acquired from Brooklyn over the winter, shook his head in wonder. "You'd think it was a Giant-Dodger double-header. Imagine what it'll be like here if we win a few games?"

"Better imagine what it'll be like if we lose a few," growled shortstop Johnny Logan. "They're liable to tear us limb from limb and ship us back to Boston."

On the side-lines warming up was Warren Spahn, scheduled to hurl against Gerry Staley of the St. Louis Cardinals. "Hey, you know, I'm nervous," he called to his receiver Del Crandall. "I don't think I've pitched in front of so many people since the World Series, back in 1948."

Crandall didn't remember how it was in 1948. There were few Braves from that pennant-winning team who remained to move with the franchise to Milwaukee. Aside from Spahn, there were only Vern Bickford, Sibby Sisti and Johnny Antonelli.

The Milwaukee version of the Braves was a young team. The undoubted psychological lift of new surroundings and enthusiastic fan support did much to account for its amazing success in 1953. In addition, however, it boasted some rapidly developing youngsters, and veteran strength gained in trades during the winter.

The pitching staff, besides Spahn, Bickford and Antonelli from the old Braves, included Max Surkont, Lew Burdette and Bob Buhl—the latter a rookie just out of military service—and several others. The shortstop—second base combination of Johnny Logan and Art Dittmer came up from the Brewers the year before; first baseman Joe Adcock was obtained from the Redlegs; third baseman Ed Mathews was a second-year man who came directly from the minors.

Outfielders Jim Pendleton and Bill Bruton were rookies; Bob Thorpe was a second-year man; Andy Pafko was bought from the Dodgers the previous winter. The catchers were veteran Walker Cooper and youngsters Ebba St. Claire and Del Crandall, the latter two doing most of the receiving.

When Spahn took the mound for his first game as a Milwaukee Brave, he did so with justifiable confidence, a feeling that was understandably lacking the year before. In the moment before the first Cardinal batter stepped up to hit, Warren turned his back on home plate and looked out at his teammates.

"I don't think I'll be losing many of those one-run extra-inning games this year," he said to himself. He didn't know how soon his optimistic prediction was to be tested, however.

The plate umpire called, "Play ball!" and Spahn turned around and went to work. He took the sign, wound up, kicked, threw—and the fast ball was good.

"Strike one!" bawled the umpire.

The crowd cheered.

"Atta boy, Spahnnie," came from the infield.

What a peculiar sensation, Spahn reflected. After years of playing before the silent, phlegmatic few in Boston, with generally uninspired support in the field, there was this. He stood quietly on the new mound at County Stadium, kneading the cover of the ball with his fingers, and allowed himself the momentary luxury of absorbing the unaccustomed sounds. He felt, rather than heard, the excited din of the crowd, the cries of encouragement from the Braves bench, the peppery chatter of the infielders behind him.

"Let's go there, Spahnnie boy!"

"No hitter in there, kid, no hitter in there!"

"Easy does it, Spahnnie. Take your time, Spahnnie boy!"

It was a nice feeling. It was baseball. He was grateful to be part of it. Warren stepped back on the rubber and returned to his task. He wound up and broke a sharp curve past the swinging bat of the Cardinal hitter.

The umpire's right hand shot up. "Ste-e-e-rike two!"

The game settled into a pitching duel—Staley, the Cardinals ace who was to win eighteen games that year, against Spahn. County Stadium's first crowd was getting its money's worth, cheering and groaning with each pitch, each hit. At the end of nine innings, the score was tied, 2–2. Spahn's optimistic thought about extra-inning games was about to be put to its first test.

As he strode to the mound to pitch the tenth inning, the crowd rose to its feet, buzzing expectantly, apprehensively.

"You'd think this game was the pennant clincher," Warren said to himself.

He set down the Cardinals in the tenth and returned to the dugout. Now, he thought, let's see whether all the excitement is worth while, or whether its going to be like last year, only with a fancy ribbon.

Staley got the first Braves batter, then Billy Bruton came up to hit. The rookie outfielder, playing his second big league game, came around on one of Staley's fast balls and drove it high and deep into the right field stands for the game-winning home run.

The County Stadium crowd went crazy. Fans leaped into the air and hugged each other with joy. Horns blew, whistles shrieked, cowbells clanged amid the cheers. The fever was infectious; as Bruton crossed home plate the Braves emptied their bench to greet him and pound him on the back. Then they fled down the dugout steps and trooped into their new clubhouse underneath the stands, whooping and hollering like Braves indeed.

In the locker room they clowned and pummeled each other rowdily as they undressed. Sibby Sisti, clad only in a towel, kept walking around in circles, muttering to himself in wonder. "You ever see anything like it? You ever see anything like it?"

Spahn walked over to Bruton and wrung his hand. "Billy boy, could I have used you last year!" he said with a grin.

Johnny Logan, the brash young shortstop, threw a towel at the pitcher. "Hey, Hooks, you better have a good excuse for not winning thirty this year!" he jibed.

Warren chuckled. "I'll settle for twenty right now."

In the manager's private office next to the clubhouse, Charley Grimm was being besieged by a battery of base-ball reporters. Suddenly "Jolly Cholly" waved his arms in mock rage. "I can't stand it in here," he bellowed. "It's too crowded!" He jumped from his chair and turned to Duffy Lewis, the team's traveling secretary.

"Duffy de Lew," he ordered with a grin, "you take this office. I'm moving in with the boys!"

Leaving Duffy de Lew, as Grimm, with his penchant for nicknaming people dubbed the secretary, he swaggered into the dressing room, the reporters at his heels. He pulled an equipment trunk away from the wall, sat down on it and folded his arms across his chest. "From now on, this is my office," he said.

The pattern was thus set for the rest of that incredible season. With rollicking Charley guiding them from the third base coaching box or his "office" in the dressing room, the Braves razzle-dazzled the league. Picked for no better than a fifth place finish, they came in second, behind the Dodgers. And until July, when Brooklyn recovered from its surprise and began playing at a .800 clip, the Braves threatened to steal the pennant.

A bitter, three-way dogfight raged for the lead during the first half of the season. Winning nine of their first eleven games, the Philadelphia Phillies became the early pace setters. Then the Braves got hot, won six straight and grabbed the lead. It was the Dodgers' turn next; they reeled off ten straight victories to shoot to the top on May 31st, but the irrepressible Braves took two out of three from Brooklyn in a series that followed its climb back into first place.

For three weeks it looked as though nobody would be able to get them out again. Spahn and Surkont, with Lew

Burdette brilliant in relief behind them, were virtually unbeatable. Billy Bruton was running the bases like a zephyr and playing center field like a reincarnation of Tris Speaker. Mathews, Adcock and Pafko were hitting home runs by the bushel. And Jolly Cholly, blithely strumming his left-handed banjo through it all, had them playing daring, aggressive baseball. They were running and taking the extra base; infielders brazenly gambled on making plays at second and third on bunts or infield taps in order to head off advancing runners.

It paid off with sixteen victories in twenty-three games, with three insane weeks spent in the intoxicating air of first place. Inevitably, the bubble burst. The rampaging Braves weren't that good; the Dodgers weren't that bad. Starting on June 21st the Milwaukee team dropped eight straight games. Three of the losses were to the Dodgers, who regained the lead and were never headed.

Third baseman Eddie Mathews and pitcher Warren Spahn made the National League All-Star team, and as if the volatile citizens of Milwaukee hadn't enough up to that point to drive them into hysteria, Spahn emerged from the game as the winning pitcher.

There wasn't much opportunity for cheering after that mid-July classic, but Milwaukee cheered on nevertheless. When the schedule resumed, the Dodgers ran away from the rest of the league, winning forty-one out of their next fifty games. On September 12th they clinched the pennant by beating the Braves, 5–2.

The remarkable thing about that first year in Milwaukee was the unflagging enthusiasm of the fans, no matter how their team happened to be faring at the moment. There was hardly a letdown in feeling when the Dodgers pocketed the pennant, except perhaps from a state of frenzy to one of mere delirium.

In the early weeks of the season, when the Braves were hot and big league baseball was a novelty to Milwaukee, eager ticket buyers were to be expected at County Stadium. However, when the team tailed off in July, instead of trailing off with it, attendance jumped. During the slump, a Milwaukee manufacturer shut down half his plant on a weekday and brought more than five hundred of his employees to County Stadium in chartered busses.

An out-of-town reporter, sent by the sports editor of his paper to check on reports of the mass baseball lunacy in Milwaukee, buttonholed the businessman outside the ball park.

"Isn't this going to rather extreme lengths to express your loyalty to the Braves?" he questioned.

The fan stared at the reporter as though he had blasphemed. "It's when our boys are losing that they really need us!" he boomed. Then he glanced impatiently at his watch. "It's late!" he gasped. "They've already started batting practice!" Wild eyed, he rushed into the ball park.

There was no end to the wonders. During a game with the Dodgers at County Stadium, a man rushed into the first-aid office, blood streaming from a gash in his head. "I ran into a post," he explained.

The nurse examined the wound. "You need stitches in that," she said.

The fan waved his arms impatiently. "Never mind the stitches!" he exclaimed. "Just patch it up fast so I can get back to the game."

The team that nobody cared to see in Boston, everybody in Milwaukee wanted to see. Nothing could keep those incredibly rabid fans away. One Sunday in May, a torrential rain washed out a scheduled double-header with the Phillies, but more than five thousand die-hards stood in the downpour for hours outside the gates, hoping the weather would clear. That same month a cold snap plunged the temperature to forty degrees for a night game with the Giants; the fans packed thermos jugs of hot coffee, bundled into their overcoats and jammed the park.

The adoration of the Braves players was limitless; there wasn't anything approaching it in baseball history. Most baseball cities have had "Days" for local favorites, when the players are given gifts by the fans. In Milwaukee, every day was a "Day" for every ballplayer.

Spahn was given a tractor for his ranch in Hartshorne, Oklahoma; Andy Pafko received a Cadillac; Sid Gordon a thousand-dollar bond, jewelry, clothes and assorted gifts. Sibby Sisti, a utility infielder, was given a thousand-dollar bond and bicycles for his four children; fans chipped in and put a down payment of five thousand dollars on a home for Bill Bruton and his family. So it went—straight down the line-up.

In addition, local business firms showered them with a continuous supply of such items as cigars, candy, cigarettes, canned goods, eggs, poultry, gas and oil for their cars, cleaning services, clothes, barber services and what have you.

Attendance figures were fantastic. After thirteen games at County Stadium, the Braves surpassed their season's total at Boston the year before. On July 31st they hit the million attendance mark; at season's end a total of 1,826,397 fans had paid their way into County Stadium, an all-time National League record.

There were times when the bubbling enthusiasm of the fans was beyond comprehension—except to other local fanatics. Every play was a big play, every game a vital one, every series crucial. A base hit by a Braves player was the signal for wild cheering. A victory meant smiling faces in the offices the next morning; a loss cast a pall of gloom over the city, and during the next game the cheering was sure to be redoubled.

Though much of the excitement may have appeared aimless, the Braves did provide their share of legitimate thrills. Eddie Mathews was the only regular to hit better than .300, but it was a slugging team nevertheless. Mathews also socked forty-seven home runs, to lead both leagues and set a new high for the club, and a new team home run record of one hundred and fifty-six was established.

Their pitching was the best in the league, with a staff earned-run average of 3.30. Spahn, flashing the finest form of his career, was the earned-run king with a 2.10 average, and he tied Robin Roberts of the Phillies for the most wins, with twenty three. Five of his victories were shutouts, one of which came close to immortalizing him in baseball history.

It happened in a game against the Phillies, at County Stadium on August 1st. Warren really had his stuff that day. When they hit the ball at all, the Philadelphia batters were bouncing it on the ground or popping it meekly into the air. Spahn retired ten men in a row, then in the fourth inning Richie Ashburn hit a high bounder to shortstop. Jim Pendleton could do nothing but wait for the ball to come down. He fielded it cleanly and threw it to first, but Ashburn, one of the fastest men in baseball, beat it out for a base hit.

Nothing significant was attached to the hit at the time. Working behind a 3–0 lead, Spahn disposed of the two batters following Ashburn to close out the fourth inning, then walked back to the dugout. He sat down next to Del Crandall.

"Well, there goes your no-hitter," the catcher grinned facetiously.

Warren grinned back. "Yeah, and a perfect game, too."

As the game wore on, both men began to realize that their derisive grins should have been rueful instead. Spahn toiled through the fifth, the sixth, the seventh— and not another enemy player reached base. When the Phils went down in order again in the eighth, a murmur of chagrin swept through the crowd, and angry glances were aimed at the press box, seeking out the anonymous official who gave Ashburn a hit instead of Pendleton an error.

The stands were silent as Warren took the mound to pitch the ninth inning. He disposed of Eddie Kazanski on a foul to Crandall. Pinch hitter Connie Ryan struck out—Spahn's eighth victim of the game. When Eddie Waitkus grounded out to end the game, the crowd rose to its feet and filled County Stadium with thunderous applause for the brilliant job of pitching they had just witnessed.

There was no whooping and hollering, however. By their refrain from such celebration, the fans were indicating to Warren their knowledge and regret that he had missed pitching a perfect no-hit game by the split second in which Ashburn had beaten that throw to first base.

Chapter Eleven ·

Warren Spahn sat alone in the Braves' clubhouse at County Stadium, sipping moodily on a bottle of soda pop. The roar of the crowd in the grandstand above reached him dimly; the game with the Giants was still going on. But it was over for him. He sighed heavily, got up from his stool and deposited the empty bottle in a rack. Then he walked over to his locker and began to undress.

Five straight, he reflected bitterly. He shook his head at the enormity of it. Five straight times knocked out of the box. Five straight losses. Spahn paused for a moment in his reflection and cocked his head at a sudden shout from the crowd in the stadium. Something must be going on, he mused. Maybe the guys can kick up a rally yet and get me off the hook. He laughed shortly to himself. "Rally," he scoffed. "Not the way we've been playing ball."

He removed his sweat-soaked uniform shirt and threw it on a pile of dirty clothes in a corner. This was supposed to be the big year, he reflected sadly. Everybody said so in spring training—the sports writers, the front office, the experts, everybody. No more of that "Always a bridesmaid and never a bride," they said. "The year 1956 will finally be the one for the Milwaukee Braves. They'll win the pennant by ten games."

Spahn snorted to himself. We'll be lucky to be even a first-division bridesmaid this year, he brooded. Where are we now, fourth place? Fifth? He didn't even look at the team standings in the papers any more. Like a guy afraid of finding his own obituary, he thought, and chuckled silently at his simile. At that, for a while he had figured he was ready for one himself back in 1954. A baseball obituary, at least. His mind sobered quickly at the memory.

The knee—the right one, it was the first time—had really started to bother him in 1953, but not enough to affect his pitching. Heck, that was his best year. The bone specialists had advised him to have the knee operated on, though, when the season was over. A couple of weeks on crutches after the operation, and he'd be as good as new, they told him. Hah! That was a great one!

Warren added his uniform pants and sweatshirt to the pile of clothes and sat down in his shorts on the stool in front of his locker cage. Man, what a rough season that 1954 started out to be, he recalled. The knee didn't heal at all the way they said it would. It felt kind of funny, sometimes stiff, sometimes weak. He tried to go easy on it, afraid the knee would buckle under the regular pounding it would have to take. That was a bad mistake. But it took him a long time to discover his error.

Spahn stood up and rummaged through the shelf in

his locker for a bar of soap. He found a fresh one and began removing the wrapper. I sometimes wonder how I ever won a game those first couple of months, he mused. His brow furrowed as he frowned at the memory. Favoring the knee made him do everything wrong. He was striding too far. He wasn't following through. He began to push the ball, aiming it instead of throwing. The hitters got to him and began belting him out of the box. Grimm turned him into a spot pitcher. He'd go once a week, maybe. His confidence began to slip. He wasn't sure he could put the ball where he wanted to any more. He was afraid to try for the corners, afraid to throw the fast balls, afraid he was through.

The troubled hurler shook his head to dispel the memory. The doctors finally examined his knee and said nothing was wrong with it. The whole thing was in his mind. There was nothing to do but find his own way out of the trap he'd made for himself. He went to catcher Del Crandall, his roomie.

"I don't know a good pitch from a bad one any more," he said to the catcher. "You gotta help me. When I throw one that's good, really good, you come right out and tell me. And don't kid me. That's the only way I'm going to find out how to throw again."

It took time, but it worked. Gradually he regained his form, his confidence. He began to throw the high hard one again—and won six straight. The Braves moved with him. From fifteen and a half games back they moved to within three games of the top. But they couldn't make it the rest of the way. Bridesmaids again, he smiled wryly to himself, trailing behind the Dodgers, who trailed behind the bride—the New York Giants.

Spahn stepped out of his shorts, slipped his feet into wooden clogs, grabbed a towel off the hook in his locker and clopped off to the shower. Well, all's well that ends well, he ruminated. Then he jerked the phrase back to mind and examined it more throughly. "Or is it?" he challenged aloud.

Sure, he continued to win after he regained his form in 1954. As a matter of fact, he lost only two games in the last ten weeks of the season, winding up with twenty-one wins and twelve losses. But in September the business with the knee started again. Only it was the left knee this time, and meant another operation in October.

He dropped the towel on a stool outside the shower and stepped into the stall. He listened for a moment to the noises from the game in the ball park. Should be the ninth inning by now, he speculated. Then he turned a handle and let the hot spray hiss against his weary body.

Good thing the hitters didn't know how bad my legs were last year, he thought after a while. They'd have bunted me right out of the league. As it was, they did a pretty good job of it, he recalled sourly. Only seventeen wins—first time he didn't win twenty with Milwaukee— and fourteen losses. Grimm was pulling him out much earlier in the game that year, too. His knees would start to stiffen along about the fifth inning.

It wasn't a particularly happy year all around. They played bridesmaid again to the Dodgers. Brooklyn opened the 1955 season by winning ten straight and nobody ever caught them. But there were grumblings. Not from the fans. Spahn smiled at the thought of Milwaukee's effervescent baseball partisans. No, they were as enthusiastic as ever. A little more sophisticated, maybe, than they were in 1953. They knew now what they had a right to expect from a pennant contender. But win or lose, they continued to break attendance records at the park.

No, the grumblings emanated from elsewhere. They came from the press and they came from the Braves' front office. The uncle and the father of the bridesmaid were impatiently waiting for her to become a bride. Well, who was more anxious than the perennial bridesmaid herself?

Spahn stepped out from under the spray and began to soap his body. Some sports writers and the front office didn't see it that way, apparently. Several times he recalled reading hints that some of the Braves were too complacent, weren't hustling. Grimm came in for his share of the blame, too. It was said he was too easygoing a manager; the players took advantage of him. Toward the end of the season there was a rumor that unless the Braves got off to a good start in 1956, Grimm would be fired. Warren's silent laugh was humorless. In that case, the skipper didn't have long to go. Here it was the second week in June—and they were flirting with the second division.

He stepped back under the shower spray and rinsed

off the soap. I sure haven't been much help myself so far, he admitted ruefully to himself. Unless we pull this one out today I'll have a three-and-six record. And five straight losses. He winced at the grim statistic, and the painful reminder of what was responsible for it. That game he lost to the Giants, the one that started this losing streak, that's when he noticed it first, he recalled. He considered then that pitching with only two days' rest might be responsible, but when the Redlegs and Pirates beat him in succession, he acknowledged the sad truth. His fast ball was gone.

Spahn turned off the shower. At first, there was a kind of numbness, he recalled, as he reached for his towel, a kind of shock that he felt about losing his fast ball. Then the feeling had turned to fear. Then desperation. Finally he even began to feel a little sorry for himself. He wondered if his loss could reasonably be compared to, say, a singer losing his voice, a violinist losing the flexibility of his fingers, an artist his sight.

He quickly realized that he was being maudlin, and at that precise moment he was on his way back. He knew that now. He recognized that his comparisons were much less than reasonable; they were ridiculous. His was not a crippling affliction; he had merely lost one weapon in an arsenal of pitching talent. True, it was his most potent weapon, but to compensate he could develop a new pitch. He *must* develop a new one.

But what kind of pitch to develop? As a fast ball pitcher primarily, he used to throw high and hard, across the chest. Now that he didn't throw hard any more, he realized he had better not throw high either, at the risk of being belted regularly for home runs. After some deliberation, he decided to develop a sinker pitch. When perfected, a sinker comes in at a batter like a ball rolling off the end of a table; it's a tough pitch to hit solidly.

Spahn finished toweling himself dry, tied the cloth around his waist and stomped back to his locker, his wooden shower clogs clap-clapping against the floor of the dressing room. For nearly two weeks he had been working on the sinker, Warren calculated. He sighed. The road back was a hard one. He opened his locker door, stowed the soap and towel and began putting on his street clothes.

He must have thrown more than one hundred sinkers in practice before he tried the first one in a game, Spahn figured. He remembered asking Del Crandall to warm him up one day, and the catcher's reaction to his first pitch. Crandall jackknifed out of his crouch, his face split in a broad grin.

"Hoho, what have we here?" the catcher sang out.

Warren smiled secretively. "Just a sign of old age. I was thirty-five a couple of weeks ago."

Crandall was curious. "You really fooling around with this thing, Hooks?"

"Fooling around with it? It's going to be my best pitch."

The catcher snorted. "You? A 'junk' pitcher?"

Spahn forced himself to grin. "It's only 'junk' when the

other pitchers throw it. When you start to throw the stuff yourself, it's called a clever assortment."

Crandall looked at him searchingly. "Hey, are you serious?"

He nodded.

"Why?"

"You caught me in enough games to know the answer to that one."

The catcher shrugged. "So you had a couple of off days."

"Off? You mean awf-ul!"

"You pitched two shutouts before you went bad," Crandall persisted.

"I thought of that, too. But it's simple. I figured I'm kind of like an old race horse now. I can flash an extra kick once—maybe twice—a year. But when this season started I thought I was still a prime colt. When I pitched those two shutouts I didn't know I was blowing a whole year's supply of fast balls."

A pained expression appeared on the catcher's face. "You really think so, Hooks? Honest?"

"I really think so."

"In that case," Crandall said, running back to squat behind the warm-up plate, "we'd better get to work."

A couple of days later he got his first chance to try the sinker in a ball game. It was quite an historic occasion, too, he recalled. Warren slipped into his trousers, laced his shoes, groped for a comb in his locker, found it and walked to the mirror hanging on a clubhouse wall. He squinted into the glass, grimaced at himself, studied critically the angles and planes of his face and the over-sized hook of his nose.

You better learn to throw a beaut of a sinker, he advised the face in the mirror, because you're never gonna be a movie star. And that's for sure.

He began combing his hair. Yeah, that was quite a historic occasion for the unveiling of my sinker, Spahn resumed his ruminating. Pitched against the Dodgers that day. First time in three years. Of course, it was only in County Stadium. He practically had to pay his way to get into Ebbets Field. Nobody had let him pitch there in nearly ten years. They all said the Dodgers murdered left-handers in Ebbets Field, that they had his number especially. He never agreed with that claim, even had a couple of minor tiffs with Grimm when the pitching rotation was obviously juggled just to keep him out of Ebbets Field. He was the butt of a lot of riding from the bench jockeys because of that. It wasn't the riding so much that bothered him, though. He could take it. But the fact wounded his pride. Heck, when he has his stuff, a good pitcher can beat any team, in any ball park.

The situation came up just a couple of weeks back, and he recalled saying that very thing to a writer from a New York paper—what was his name—Gross. Milt Gross. From the *Post*. They were sitting around in the Braves' dressing room at Ebbets Field, just the two of them, because the game had already started. Gross asked him if it was true that even some of his own teammates were beginning to ride him about his virtual banishment from the Ebbets Field pitching mound.

It was true. After the last game at Pittsburgh, while the Braves were packing their gear for this trip to Brooklyn, one of his teammates called out to him, "Hey Spahnnie, where you going for your three-day vacation?" It was good-natured needling, but it was not the first time he had had to take it from a Braves player.

Spahn patted a few rebellious hairs into place with his hand, nodded with satisfaction at the reflection of his handiwork in the wall mirror and returned to his locker. Then he zippered open a canvas overnight bag and removed a shirt.

He told Gross how he felt about the whole thing. The bench jockeying was not important. He was a big league pitcher and he pitched when he was told. But he was piling up some creditable records next to his name. He had a right to take pride in his reputation. But he felt that he'd always be remembered as the pitcher who couldn't beat the Dodgers.

Maybe Grimm read the story Gross wrote in the *Post*, Spahn reflected ruefully. Maybe that's why Charley gave him his first start against them in three years, even if it was only at County Stadium. Just his luck that he got this opportunity to prove himself after he lost his fast ball, and before he had time to perfect his new sinker. He didn't get a chance to throw many sinkers against the Dodgers that day, or a chance to throw much of anything, as a matter of fact. The Dodgers knocked him out of the box before he even had a chance to work up a sweat.

That was his fourth straight loss—and today's game was going to be his fifth straight unless the Braves came up with some runs. The sinker was working a little better today, however, and that was something to be encouraged about, at least. He sighed wistfully, remembering how things used to be, then reached into his locker for a necktie.

He was back at the mirror, drawing the knot in his tie, when he heard a roar from the stadium, and a moment later the players began trooping into the dressing room. One look at their faces—and he knew he didn't have to ask.

The Braves and Warren Spahn had just lost another one.

Three days later he got another chance to try his sinker, this time on the Giants. Spahn's normal pitching rotation called for more than two days' rest, but this was the last game of the Braves' home stand, and the first stop on their road trip was Ebbets Field. It was vacation time for Spahn again.

In the Milwaukee dressing room after that getaway game with the Giants, Warren was getting his usual needling about the trip to Brooklyn. But he met it all with a broad grin. Mixing his new sinker with two different curves and a change-up, he struck out ten Giants that day, winning his first game in almost a month, 5–2. Now he felt a new confidence stirring within him. Unless his performance had been a fluke, it proved that he could be a winner again, even without a fast ball. As the Braves boarded their plane that evening for the trip east, Warren felt himself chafing with impatience.

Nuts to the Dodgers, he thought. Bring on the rest of the league!

Chapter Twelve ·

When Warren strolled out to the mound at the Polo Grounds five days later, he was playing for a new manager. On June 16th, when the Braves were still in Brooklyn, Jolly Cholly Grimm, more grim that day than jolly, announced his resignation, and coach Fred Haney was given the helm of the floundering Milwaukee team.

It was undoubtedly pure coincidence that the Braves took off on an eleven-game winning streak the day Haney took over. The team wasn't playing any harder to win for him than they used to for Grimm. If anything, the opposite was more likely. Jolly Cholly had been a popular skipper, and though they were happy about their win streak, several players expressed regret that it had come at a time to make Grimm look so bad—and Haney so good.

Warren won two of those eleven victories, beating the Giants, 2–1, and the Pirates, 3–2. His three straight wins gave him a 6–6 record going into July. By that time word was getting around to the hitters of the National League that although Spahn wasn't as fast as he used to be, he was trickier.

Under manager Fred Haney, life was different for the Braves. There were more clubhouse meetings, more strategy discussions, less horseplay. On the field, Haney took complete charge. No player stole on his own or swung on his own; orders were flashed from the manager's post in the dugout.

It wasn't a completely grim existence, however. Particularly for Warren. A conscientious, dedicated player who required no watchdog to keep him in shape and at the peak of pitching form, he got along well with Haney, probably better than he did with any manager he played under previously.

When the Braves were at County Stadium, Warren's wife Lorene often came up from the ranch in Hartshorne to see them play, bringing with her their seven-year-old son, Gregory. The wartime secretary who once didn't know home plate from a double play was by now a rabid baseball fan; as much as she loved the Oklahoma ranch, where she and Warren were raising a growing herd of beef cattle, Lorene couldn't stay away from the Milwaukee ball park for too long.

On days when Spahn was not scheduled to pitch, she came to the playing field before game time and deposited young Gregory with his father. "Now you take care of Greg today, Warren," she said. "You know I like to keep score during the game, and he interrupts me with too many questions."

And Spahn laughed. "Where do you suggest I keep him? In the bat rack?"

Often as not, young Gregory ended up in the bullpen

with his father. And when the Braves were winning and the bullpen brigade relaxed, the pitchers played catch with the overjoyed youngster. The first time this happened, Lew Burdette noticed that Greg threw the ball with his left hand.

"Aha!" the pitcher exclaimed. "Look what we've got here. Another lefthander in the Spahn family!"

Warren grinned. "To tell you the truth, Lew, he's not really a lefthander. That is, he's not a natural born lefthander, like I am. His right arm was burned in an accident at home a few years back, and he began to use his left most of the time. He's been a lefthander ever since."

"Who cares what kind of lefthander he is," Burdette growled good-humoredly. "He's still a lefthander, isn't he?" He stooped and patted the boy's shoulder. "You're going to be a great pitcher like your Daddy someday, aren't you, Greg?"

Gregory Spahn nodded proudly, but his father shook his head. "Not Warren Spahn's boy. No pitching for him. Pitchers work too hard, harder than anybody else in a ball game. And they're too fragile. A blister on the finger and you're out of work. A pain in the shoulder and you can have a bad year. How many promising kids never got past a tryout camp because they mysteriously developed a sore arm? How many big league pitchers had their careers suddenly ended by a chip in the elbow, a pain in the shoulder, or by a sore arm that no doctor could even diagnose? Look what almost happened to me?"

Burdette looked at him, surprised. "You sound like you mean it."

Spahn nodded. "I do. I'm not bitter. But I think a youngster stands a better chance of making it to the big leagues and staying there if he's not a pitcher. And if Greg here wants to play baseball, that's the way I'm going to aim him."

Burdette grinned suddenly. "Yeah, well I'm giving two-to-one little Gregory boy here winds up on the mound like his old man."

The seriousness was gone then, and the two men laughed. Greg, who had listened to his father only half understanding, laboriously picked up a bat and called to him, "C'mon, Dad, pitch the ball in and I'll knock it a mile."

The youngster was holding the heavy bat in an awkward cross-handed grip, and when Burdette saw this he burst into a loud guffaw. "Look at the way your boy's holding that bat, Spahnnie," he said. "He sure doesn't look like a home run hitter to me. If you want him to be a ball player, you'd better teach him how to pitch."

Not all the Braves were so happy, however. While there were many who prospered under the strict guidance of manager Haney, there were many, too, who resented the new era of discipline. For his part, the Milwaukee skipper was intensely concerned about his team's intolerably casual attitude toward the pennant race.

"They're spoiled rotten!" he confided to a Milwaukee sports writer. "But there's just so much I can do about it without causing serious trouble. It's different when you take charge of a team in spring training; you can get things to be the way you think they should. But in midseason . . ." he shook his head despairingly.

The preseason experts predicted that 1956 would be the pennant year for Milwaukee, but apparently everybody regarded the prediction seriously except the players themselves. It was widely conceded later that up until the month of September the Braves did not consider they had a chance to win. It was small wonder, then, that when they woke up early that month and found the pennant practically lying in their laps, they didn't know how to wrap it up.

It was apparent by July that the National League pennant race was going to be a hot one among the Braves, the Dodgers and the Cincinnati Redlegs. On July 12th the Braves began a four-game sweep of the Dodgers to gain the league lead, and they didn't relinquish it until September 15th. As late as Labor Day they held a three- and one-half-game lead over Brooklyn and the Redlegs, but their complacency and nonchalance was so imperturable that they were able to watch the pennant slip slowly through their fingers without any apparent concern about the impending tragedy—until it was too late.

For all their lackadaisical attitude, it took a heartbreaking, twelve-inning loss to the Cardinals on the next to the last day of the season to beat the Braves.

The scoreboard at Busch Stadium in St. Louis the night of September 29th exhibited the grim news that the Dodgers won a double-header from the Pirates during the day, giving them a half-game hold on first place.

With their backs to the wall by this time, the Braves' carefree air had changed to apprehension. They never expected to get so close to winning the pennant; now that they were so close to losing it, the pressure twisted them into tortured knots.

The calmest man in the house that night at St. Louis was probably Warren Spahn, the one who had the heaviest load to bear. Scheduled to oppose Herman Wehmeier, Warren knew how much rode on his left arm—if the Braves lost, they'd be one game behind with one game to go. The best they could hope for then would be a tie, and the Dodgers would have to lose their final contest for that.

He brought a twenty and ten record into the game, a remarkable comeback from his early season low mark of three wins and six losses. During the heat of the race, when the rest of the Milwaukee pitching staff faltered, Spahn came through with an amazing streak of hurling; since August 3rd he had lost only one game, while winning ten.

As he took the mound to pitch the first inning, Warren might well have thought he was in Milwaukee, instead of St. Louis. Hundreds of fans had journeyed from the Braves' home city to cheer them on in the vital series with the Cardinals. And they were joined in their rooting by the St. Louis citizens, avid Dodger haters for many years.

For the first five innings Spahn was untouchable; not a Cardinal got a hit. The Braves squeezed one run out of Wehmeier, meanwhile, giving Warren a 1–0 lead going into the home half of the sixth. He retired the first two men, but successive doubles erased his no-hitter, his shutout and his lead.

The score remained 1–1 through the eleventh inning. While the Cardinals got only four more hits off Spahn after the sixth, the Braves were continually wasting good scoring chances. By the twelfth inning the fans were hoarse from screaming; the tension in the ball park was overwhelming.

The Braves couldn't score in the twelfth, and Spahn stalked out of the dugout to pitch to the Cardinals. He retired the first batter, then Stan Musial came up to the plate. Working him carefully, Warren brought the count to two balls and two strikes. Then Musial hit a soft fly ball that just dropped between Bruton and Aaron for a double. Kenny Boyer was walked intentionally to set up a double play situation.

Rip Repulski stepped in to hit. Spahn went into his stretch, checked the runners, then slipped a curve over for a strike. Another curve was too low. The crowd was standing now, holding its breath with each pitch.

Repulski swung at a change-up, and it was strike two. A good spot for a sinker, Warren calculated. With two strikes he's going to be a little anxious, and if he does hit the ball, it will be on the ground and we could get the double play.

He shook off his catcher's sign until he got the sinker signal. He nodded, stepped up on the mound, stretched, looked back at the base runners and threw the sinker to the plate. Overanxious, as Spahn had figured, Repulski lunged at the sinking pitch, hitting it sharply on the ground to third.

It worked! Warren thought, but as he turned to follow the play he saw the ball carom off Ed Mathews' knee and roll into left field. Repulski ran out the hit for a double, as Musial scored the winning run.

Spahn stood rooted to the mound, stunned by the sudden defeat. Finally he walked slowly off the field toward the Braves' dugout. Manager Haney came out to meet him at the first base line, and as the crowd voiced its thundering approval, he shook Warren's hand. His skipper's simple act of warm commiseration broke down Spahn's stoic reserve. With Haney's arm around his shoulders and the sympathetic cheers of the crowd sounding in his ears, Warren walked the rest of the way to the dugout, weeping unashamedly.

In the St. Louis clubhouse after the game the Cardinal players sat around in their uniforms, still awed by Spahn's pitching performance. Wehmeier, the winning pitcher, shook his head sadly. "This is the first time in my life I ever felt sorry for a man who pitched against me," he said. "Spahn was terrific, much better than I was."

Outfielder Wally Moon sat staring vacantly in front of him, as though he could still see Warren's lanky form going through its wondrous motions on the mound.

"He's just the greatest pitcher in baseball, that's all," Moon said at last.

Though there was still one game to play before the Braves could actually lose the pennant, the gloom of their locker room at St. Louis left no doubt about their hopes for a tie. They went through the motions of playing again the next day, beating the Cardinals. But the Dodgers won their game with the Pirates, to take the pennant.

Later that year, the Milwaukee Baseball Writers Association picked Spahn as the most valuable player on the 1956 Braves, and awarded him their Manning Vaughan Memorial Plaque. It was a distinguished honor, and Warren accepted it proudly at the baseball writers' dinner in January. But everyone knew that he would have traded a roomful of personal awards for one base hit at the right time in that epochal disaster in St. Louis.

Chapter Thirteen ·

For all practical purposes, the 1957 baseball campaign of the Milwaukee Braves began within five minutes after the final curtain to their disastrous swan dive exhibition of 1956. After beating the Cardinals in the meaningless aftermath to Warren Spahn's epic defeat, the Braves gathered in their dressing room at Busch Stadium for a post-mortem meeting with manager Fred Haney. If they were expecting anything like the usual wait-till-next-year pap from their tough little skipper they were quickly disabused of that notion. After their bush league collapse under the heat of the recent pennant fight, if there were still a few Braves with a drop of complacency in their blood, Haney shed it with the first slash of his razor-edged speech of warning.

He stomped into the center of the dressing room and stood there for several silent moments surveying his dispirited ball team, his flint-keen eyes flicking from man to man in unsparing excoriation. Finally he told them to stop what they were doing and listen to him for a few seconds; he had a little something to say to them, short and sweet.

"You had a good time this year, boys," Haney said when he gained their attention. "And I want you to have a good time this winter. Because when you see me again next spring, you're going to meet the nastiest so-and-so you ever ran into."

That was all. Haney left them then and returned to his office. The Milwaukee ballplayers looked at each other in mute understanding, then continued packing their equipment for the flight home that evening.

There was very little conversation during the plane ride to Milwaukee. The unhappy Braves just wanted to get back to County Stadium, pick up their belongings and get away as fast as they could. As their plane circled Billy Mitchell Field for the landing, they could see a vast crowd gathered below. The Braves exchanged nervous glances. They were justifiably apprehensive. Considering all the newspaper stories accusing them of choking up under pressure and blowing the pennant, they couldn't be sure the crowd had not come to jeer them out of town. They were far wrong.

As they walked hesitantly down the ramp from the plane, the crowd surged forward. There were thousands of them—men, women and children, even women with children in their arms. The fans surrounded the players. Some of them were crying. Many were shouting words of encouragement and sympathy. The Braves made their way slowly through the gauntlet of well-wishing citizens, pausing here and there along the way to accept a pat on the back, to shake an outstretched hand, to exchange a few words with one of their loyal followers.

Outside the airlines terminal, busses chartered by the Chamber of Commerce waited to ride the team into town. The crowd retreated through the gates of the airport, spilling out and overflowing into the streets as it swirled around and engulfed the Braves' vehicles. The players began to board the busses. Warren Spahn exchanged a final handclasp with one of the fans and turned to go. Just then a little girl broke loose from her mother's hand and ran up to the Milwaukee hurler.

"Don't worry, Mr. Spahn," the little girl cried. "Next year is going to be a lucky one for all of us."

Luck was not a factor taken into consideration, however, when the Braves began spring training in 1957. Manager Fred Haney greeted his players in Florida as he had parted from them in St. Louis five months before.

"I want you guys to get one thing straight from the beginning," he told them. "I don't care what any of you think about me or say about me. I just want to make you guys better ballplayers. By the time this season is over, everyone of you is going to hate my guts. But you'll be cashing your World Series checks by then. So it won't matter."

It may well be, as one Milwaukee sports writer suggested after that 1957 season, that "all the Braves ever needed was a manager who carried a sandbag instead of a banjo." The exaggerated references to Fred Haney and Charley Grimm were a sports writer's literary license, of course. At the same time, it was more truth than poetry.

The Milwaukee club leaped from the barrier like a race horse stung by a jockey's whip. Spahn lead the charge with a victory on opening day—and the Braves were off and running as they never ran before. In two weeks, as they won nine of their first ten ball games, Haney's fired-up crew had baseball experts asking, "Who's going to stop the Braves?"

It wasn't only the fact of their winning, but rather the manner of their winning, that clearly exposed the difference between this Milwaukee team and its practically identical counterpart which had sailed blithely into disaster the year before. Five of the Braves' first nine victories were by one-run margins; their only loss was by one run—in ten innings. Four times they had to come from behind to win. They were playing aggressive, confident ball, hanging on, ready to exploit a break, not giving up until the final out.

You couldn't discourage them. The year before, when they were behind in the late stages of a ball game, they were too ready to shrug off the game with a "tomorrow's another day" philosophy. Not now. The Cardinals led them in one game, 2–0. They got a run back to make it 2–1. The Cardinals opened the gap, 4–1. The Braves rallied to tie the game, 4–4. But again the Cardinals broke loose, 7–4. The Braves didn't quit, but kept hacking away until they won the game, 8–7.

It was difficult to believe this was the team that had been just playing along for the ride a year earlier. There were the same faces, the same uniforms with the same numbers. Joe Adcock was on first, Danny O'Connell on second, Ed Mathews on third, Johnny Logan at short-stop. Billy Bruton still roamed center field, flanked by Bobby Thomson and Hank Aaron. Del Crandall was the number one catcher again, and the mound staff was headed by Spahn, Burdette and Buhl, followed by Gene Conley, Taylor Phillips, Bob Murff, Ray Crone and Ernie Johnson.

The players readily acknowledged the change in themselves and in the team.

"We're playing smarter baseball this year," Del Crandall offered.

Shortstop Johnny Logan nodded. "That's Haney. He's the toughest guy I ever met in baseball—and the more you're with him the meaner he gets. But he's teaching us more about the game than any of us ever knew before."

"The big difference as I see it," added Bob Buhl, "is that everybody wants to help out the team, instead of every guy looking out for himself."

Logan agreed. "But there's more," he said. "Last year at this time there wasn't one guy around here who thought we were going anywhere. This year there isn't one of us who doesn't think we have what it takes to win the pennant."

One week after his thirty-sixth birthday, Warren Spahn won his fourth straight game of the season, a ten-inning victory over the Giants, and in the clubhouse after the game the Braves were kidding him about his age.

"Hey, Hooks," Logan called to him across the locker

room, "tell the truth. Aren't you really older than Satchel Paige?"

"Yeah, Spahnnie, when are you gonna retire and give some younger guys a chance to play?" Crandall kidded him.

Warren grinned at them. "If all I had to do was pitch to hitters like you two guys, I could play for another forty years."

The Braves were by no means running away from the rest of the league, despite their big jump gained in the first two weeks. The Redlegs, the Cardinals and the Dodgers were right behind them. Through the spring months and all through July the entire first division was locked in a close struggle for the league lead. At times no more than three games separated the league leader from the fourth-place club. Losing one game often dropped a team two positions in the standings. A round of Sunday double-headers could scramble the picture of the whole division.

Many baseball experts and sports writers privately conceded the pennant to the Braves after June 15th, however. On that day they obtained second baseman Red Schoendienst from the Giants in a trade for pitcher Ray Crone, infielder Danny O'Connell and outfielder Bobby Thomson. A thirty-four-year-old veteran who was the National League's All-Star second baseman eight times, Schoendienst took charge of the Milwaukee infield and molded it into a smoothly operating unit. He was not only a superb fielder, but owned a reputation as one of the league's toughest hitters in the clutch.

Everything seemed to be breaking right for the Braves. Even Warren Spahn's luck. He was in bed in a New York hotel one night, in an exhausted sleep after beating the Giants that evening, when his phone rang urgently. He heard the ringing in his sleep, but tried to ignore it. Insistently, the phone jangled loudly in the stillness of the room. Warren grudgingly climbed out of the depths of his slumber; he shook himself awake and squinted through sticking eyelashes at the clock on the table at his bedside. Three o'clock.

Three o'clock! His head jerked erect, startled. Who in blazes would be idiotic enough to call him at three o'clock in the morning! The phone shrieked on as he stared at it, stupefied with wonder and sleep. He turned in his bed and looked over at his roommate, Lew Burdette. "Atom bomb couldn't wake him," Warren mumbled to himself, and stretched his arm out for the phone.

"Hello," he croaked sleepily into the mouthpiece.

"Warren! Warren! We've struck oil! Oil!" It was his wife Lorene, calling from their ranch in Hartshorne.

Spahn was still only partly awake. "That's nice dear," he said. "I'm glad you called. How's Greg?"

"Warren! Don't you understand what I'm telling you? We've struck oil? Remember that piece of land we leased for extra grazing this year? Well, I was told to do some drilling there, but I didn't want to tell you and get you anxious about it until something happened for sure. And tonight it happened! We've struck oil! Warren! Warren! Do you hear me?"

Spahn's eyes were closed and his head was nodding.

"Yes, dear, I hear you. Oil. Very good. I'm glad you called. Goodnight, dear. Kiss Greg for me. I'll call you tomorrow maybe."

He hung up on Lorene's frantic voice, lay down in his bed and buried his head in the pillow. For several moments he was still, dozing off. Suddenly he jerked upright, wide awake. "Oil!" he cried. "Oil!" He leaped out of bed and ran around the room aimlessly. He picked up the phone and dropped it again. He wanted to do something, but he didn't know what. "Oil, oil," he repeated to himself as he whirled around. Then he stopped and stared at the slumbering form of his roommate. "How can he sleep at a time like this?" he exclaimed.

Warren bounded to Burdette's bed and shook the pitcher's body violently. "Wake up! Wake up, Lew!" he cried. "I've struck oil! You hear me! I've struck oil! Wake up!"

Burdette turned over slowly and half opened his eyes. "What happened? What time is it?"

Spahn danced up and down in front of him. "We've struck oil, Lew! On the ranch! Oil!"

Burdette stared at him glazedly. "I don't care if you just inherited the United States Mint," he growled grumpily. "I still gotta pitch tomorrow, so shut up and let me sleep."

With that, he let his head fall back on the pillow. But in a moment he too bounced up, wide awake. "Hey! Did you say oil? Real oil?"

Warren nodded gleefully. "Lorene just called me." Then he remembered. "Hey! I hung up on her. She must think I'm nuts!" He bounded to the phone. "Operator, I want to make a long distance call to Hartshorne, Oklahoma. Mrs. Lorene Spahn." He turned to Burdette. "This is the clincher, Lew," he said excitedly. "This is the tip-off. I feel it in my bones. This is my lucky year, and it's going to be lucky for all of us, the way that little girl told me at the airport last year. We're going to win the pennant. I know it."

He spoke into the phone again. "That's right operator. Hartshorne. To Mrs. Lorene Spahn. Person to person."

Burdette was grinning at him. "Well, even if we don't win, now that you're an oil tycoon, who cares?"

Spahn snorted. "Oil tycoon, nothing. I'm telling you, Lew, this time we're going to take the pennant. And the World Series, too."

On the sixth of August, the Braves simultaneously regained the league lead from the Cardinals and began a ten-game winning streak. At the same time, too, the Cardinals hit a nine-game losing streak. To further the coincidence, both streaks were stopped at the same time when the St. Louis club beat Milwaukee on August 16th. By then the Braves' lead had swelled to eight and a half games.

It wasn't smooth sailing the rest of the way, however. In September the Braves hit a sudden slump, and the terrible specter of the previous September's debacle came back to haunt them.

On the first of the month they still led the league by seven games. Spahn won his seventh in a row that day, and his seventeenth of the year.

Three days later he beat the Cubs, 8–0, with the forty-first shutout of his career, a new record for National League left-handers.

Then the Braves began to nose-dive. They dropped three straight before Spahn halted the descent temporarily by beating the Cubs, 7–2, for his ninth straight victory and nineteenth of the season. The dive resumed. Even Warren couldn't win. Twice he went after his twentieth win and twice he was denied. The Braves' lead was cut to two and a half games.

The Cardinals were putting the pressure on now, waiting for them to crack as they did in 1956. But the Braves didn't panic this time. They didn't resign themselves to second place. They went out on the ball field every day and played their hearts out, waiting for the tide to turn in their favor.

The Dodgers, out of contention at that stage of the race, gave them a hand. The Braves were holding a three-game lead. Then Brooklyn stopped a Cardinal streak with a 6–1 victory, while the Braves were beating the Giants. That extended Milwaukee's lead to four games, with only nine left to play. The Cardinals were not quitting either, however. They pulled a game out of the fire in extra innings the next day, but Spahn beat the Cubs for his twentieth victory to keep the Braves' lead at four games.

Three days later, they clinched the pennant when Hank Aaron broke up a 2–2 tie game with a home run in the eleventh inning, a victory typical of the fighting Braves of 1957. As the slugging Milwaukee outfielder trotted around the bases with his pennant-winning hit, County Stadium erupted in a volcano of sound. A thunderous roar tore from forty-five thousand pennant-hungry throats. The Braves leaped out of their dugout and grabbed Aaron when he crossed home plate. They hugged him and pounded his back, pushing and elbowing each other out of the way to get in close enough to shake his hand. Then they lifted him high in the air and bore him in joy and triumph back to their clubhouse.

Milwaukee's rabid citizens had a whole week in which to work themselves up to a fever pitch for the World Series. The normal routine of the entire city seemed to stop in favor of discussion and preparation for the coming battle with the American League flag winners, the New York Yankees. Delegations of fans were organized into rooting sections to accompany the Braves on their invasion of Yankee Stadium. Offices and factories worked out split shifts or prepared to close entirely for the games to be played at County Stadium. A city councilman proposed that the schools be closed and World Series week be declared a holiday.

The Yankees clinched their pennant on the same day the Braves did, so both teams were well rested and their pitching staffs ready. Manager Casey Stengel named his ace left-hander Whitey Ford as the Yankees' starter for the opening game in New York; Fred Haney countered with his southpaw star Warren Spahn.

The two lefties engaged in a scoreless duel for four innings. Ford cut down the first seven Braves to face him before Del Crandall singled harmlessly in the third. But the Yankees threatened to knock Warren out of the box in the first inning, when Gil McDougald and Mickey Mantle singled with one out. He bore down hard to get Bill Skowron and Yogi Berra.

Spahn gave up just one more hit before Jerry Coleman opened the home half of the fifth with a single to left. Tony Kubek then tapped a slow ground ball back to the mound. Warren pounced on it, but he had to make his play to first base as Coleman went sliding into second. Pitcher Ford flied out to Adcock, but Hank Bauer belted Spahn's first pitch up the alley in right center field. Coleman charged around third and scored easily as Aaron chased the ball all the way to the bleacher wall. Bauer wound up on second, but McDougald grounded out to end the inning.

The Yankees weren't hitting Warren very hard, but hard enough to have Haney warm up his bull pen. Then Elston Howard singled with one out in the sixth, and when Berra walked, Haney called time and walked to the mound.

"How you feeling, Spahnnie?" he asked the pitcher.

"Okay. I was a little too careful with Berra there, I think."

"Still got all your stuff?"

Warren nodded.

Haney left him and trotted back to the dugout. But he was barely settled on the bench before be bounced up again. Andy Carey hit Spahn's second pitch for a single, scoring Howard and sending Berra to third. On his way out to the mound, the Milwaukee manager waved to the bull pen for relief pitcher Ernie Johnson.

Bitterly disappointed at being knocked out in his first World Series appearance since 1948, Warren walked morosely off the mound and retired to the Braves' clubhouse.

The Yankees picked up another run that inning on a squeeze bunt by Coleman, and the Braves could get but one off Ford all day, for a 3–1 New York victory.

Despite the fact that they knocked Spahn out of the game, the Yankee players were high in praise of the Milwaukee left-hander. "The only ball we really hit hard was Bauer's double," Stengel said after the game. "I'm sure glad we don't have to face that fella all year."

With the Braves' best pitcher an early victim, some of the baseball oracles predicted a Yankee sweep in four games. That prediction was shattered the next day, however, when Lew Burdette beat Bobby Shantz, 4–2, to knot the series.

County Stadium was decked out in colorful bunting when the scene switched to Milwaukee for the third game. But before the first inning was over, it appeared that crepe would have been a more appropriate decoration. The Yankees sent Bob Buhl to the showers before he could get the side out in the first, then went on to clobber three more Braves pitchers in a 12–3 rout, one of the worst in World Series history.

Spahn was given his second chance in the fourth game. The Yankees again rocked him in the first inning. Kubek opened the game with a bunt single and moved to second on Bauer's ground out. Mickey Mantle then slammed a line drive right back to the mound. Warren knocked the ball down, whirled and got Kubek out between second and third, while Mantle legged it safely to first. Berra walked, moving Mantle to second, and McDougald singled to score Mantle for a 1–0 lead. Warren was angry at himself now. Grimly he went to work. He got Elston Howard for the third out of the inning, then got the next ten men in a row before Coleman tapped him for a single in the fifth. By then the Braves had gone out in front with a four-run rally in the fourth, on a three-run home run by Hank Aaron, followed one out later by Frank Torre's home run.

The score was still 4–1, with Spahn hurling a smooth six-hitter, when the Yankees came to bat in the ninth. Grim, deliberate, determined to win, Warren opened the inning by getting Hank Bauer on an easy fly ball to center field. When Mantle grounded out to Logan at shortstop, the fans rose and began to head for the exits.

They barely paused on their way down the aisles when Berra singled, but they stopped in their tracks when Mc-Dougald followed with another hit that flew just inches over Schoendienst's upstretched glove. That made Elston Howard, moving in to the batter's box, the potential tying run.

Manager Haney came off the bench and trotted out to the mound. The fans yelled at him. They wanted Spahn to remain in the game, to go all the way for his victory. But Haney didn't go out to remove Warren;

there was something important he wanted to remind his pitcher about.

"One thing to remember with this guy, Spahnnie," he cautioned, "don't pitch him inside where he can pull the ball. He's got a lot of power, but he needs an inside pitch to make use of it."

Warren nodded. "I'll keep it away, Skip."

Haney gave him a reassuring pat and the crowd roared its approval as he walked back to the dugout.

Spahn stepped up on the mound and went to work. He took the sign from Crandall, stretched, looked back at Berra and McDougald and threw to the plate. The pitch was good, for strike one. A curve was low for a ball. Another curve was outside, ball two. Warren took a deep breath, steadied himself and fed Howard a sinker. The Yankee first baseman swung and missed. Strike two! One out away from victory! The crowd was on its feet, shouting encouragement to the popular Milwaukee pitcher.

Spahn stepped back on the rubber, went into a slow stretch, checked the base runners, and threw a fast curve that just missed. Ball three. The crowd groaned.

Three and two now—and Howard represented the tying run. Warren blew out his breath through tight lips. Then he threw Howard a fast curve—and winced as the ball sped for the plate. He had a feeling it was heading where it wasn't supposed to go. Then his heart sank as he saw the Yankee hitter's bat flash at the pitch that was too far inside, where he had been warned not to throw.

There came the sharp, clean crack of the bat and the

ball sailed high and far over the left field fence for a home run. The game was tied, 4–4!

Spahn retired Andy Carey, to end the inning, but few fans thought he would come out to pitch the tenth. Manager Haney stayed with him, however. It was a gamble, for his pitcher had apparently tired suddenly, and two good relief men were ready in the bull pen. But Haney thought Spahn could make it—and who knows but that the manager's decision might have been affected by emotion? The Milwaukee skipper was hard as nails, but he knew how much it meant to Warren to stay in the game, to redeem himself, to earn the victory.

Haney's gamble looked like a good one when Spahn got Jerry Coleman on a ground-out and struck out Tommy Byrne. But with two out, it happened again. Kubek beat out a slow roller to second and Hank Bauer blasted a tremendous triple to score him. The Yankees were in front, 5–4, and it appeared that not only would Spahn have to take his second World Series loss, but that manager Haney would be answering to the second guessers for a long time on why he kept Spahn in the game after Howard's homer.

And still he went along with his ace left-hander. Spahn, his shoulders sagging and his heart heavy, got Mantle on a fly ball to Pafko for the third out. But there wasn't much hope left in him when he walked back to the bench. He sat down wearily and buried his face in his arms. He felt a hand nudge his shoulder. He looked up. It was Johnny Logan. The shortstop was smiling grimly. "We're not licked yet, Hooks," he said.

Spahn gulped hard and nodded. He raised his head and looked out at the field. Nippy Jones was going up to pinch-hit for him to lead off the Braves' half of the tenth.

On the first pitch, Jones was hit on the foot. Felix Mantilla went in to run for him. Bob Grim replaced Byrne on the mound for the Yankees. Schoendienst sacrificed Mantilla to second. Logan stepped into the batter's box and called out to Spahn in the Milwaukee dugout. "Here goes one for you, Hooks!"

He made good his promise. With a count of two balls and no strikes, Logan ripped a line drive down the left field line for a double. Mantilla, the fleet-footed outfielder, scooted around third like a frightened rabbit and crossed the plate with the tying run.

The crowd was screaming when Eddie Mathews walked up to hit. The din in County Stadium was deafening. Mathews hit a foul ball down the right field line. Then he fouled one down the left field line. Grim missed with two pitches, trying to get the Braves' slugger to bite at a bad ball. The next pitch was good—too good; Mathews belted it over the fence in right center field. County Stadium was a madhouse of yelling fans. The Braves rushed out of the dugout, Spahn in the lead, to meet Mathews in celebration as he crossed the plate behind Logan to give Milwaukee a dramatic 7–5 victory.

After that spine-tingling finish, the rest of the World Series seemed almost anticlimactic. Lew Burdette won his second game of the classic the next day, 1–0, to bring the Braves within one victory of the World's Championship. But that was a crown the Yankees were too accustomed to wearing to give up easily. Back on their home grounds again, they beat Bob Buhl, 3–2, sending the series to its final game.

Spahn was named by Haney as his starter; but the pitcher had to be content with seeing the finale of the 1957 World Series on television—from his bed in a New York hotel. He was sick with the flu.

Lew Burdette, who had beaten the Yankees twice, was forced to pitch with only one day's rest. But he came through with his second straight shutout of the New Yorkers, 5–0, and his third series victory. The Braves were the World's Champions!

The team returned to Milwaukee that evening to be greeted with a celebration unequaled in the history of sports. Victorious armies in the days of Julius Caesar might have been met with such wild acclaim. But never before a baseball team. Twenty thousand people swarmed over the airport waiting for the planeload of ballplayers. In the middle of town, where city officials planned a parade and formal ceremonies, two hundred and fifty thousand more were pressed like sardines into an area of perhaps two square blocks.

As the Braves plane circled the field and glided in for its landing, television crews and newsreel cameramen pressed forward. Finally the silvery transport touched down and taxied to the edge of the crowd. A ramp was wheeled to the side of the plane. When the door opened and manager Fred Haney appeared, the crowd exploded through the police barriers with a roar of greeting. Forgotten were formal ceremonies; the television crew and the cameramen were run over and swamped by thousands of frantic feet.

All through the night, until dawn of the next day, the city of Milwaukee celebrated. Brass bands marched through the streets, followed by thousands of prancing, horn-tooting revelers. Caravans of automobiles honked their way through the shrieking crowds. There were hot dogs and soda pop to be bought in the streets, and balloons and souvenirs galore.

The gray light of morning was in the eastern sky when the Braves finally broke away from the colossal victory party. They fled back to the sanctuary of their hotel, disheveled, dirty and tired, but unutterably happy.

It was time, the next afternoon, for the final quiet meeting in the Braves' clubhouse in County Stadium. The players packed their belongings and chatted about the coming winter; the hunting and fishing trips, the work to be done around the house, the business ventures to be looked after. The baseball writers were there, too, to say their good-bys to the team, to gather their last interviews until training would begin in the spring.

The players drifted out of the dressing room; Mathews, Logan, Crandall, Pafko and Covington. Bob Buhl shook hands all around and left; then Joe Adcock, and Hank Aaron, who was later to be named the National League's Most Valuable player.

The clubhouse was thinning out. There was Spahn, old Hooks himself, packing a bag. Thirty-six years old—

and the only man in the league to win twenty games in 1957. He won twenty-one and lost eleven, as a matter of fact. It was the eighth time he had a season of twenty wins or better. No left-hander in the National League ever had that many twenty-game seasons before. Only one left-hander in history ever had—the incomparable Lefty Grove.

In another month, Spahn would be getting the Cy Young Memorial Award, as the major leagues' outstanding pitcher of 1957. There weren't many records and awards left for him to aim at. The Hall of Fame? There was no doubt that he would make that, too, after he retired from baseball. But retire was a word Spahn didn't like to hear. He told a reporter before the World Series that he thought he had a couple of good years left in his arm, and then—well, maybe he would like to become a manager.

As Warren shut his locker door and turned to leave the Braves' clubhouse, one of the Milwaukee sports writers walked over to say good-by.

"I've been sitting here and thinking, Spahnnie," the man said. "There isn't much left in the way of records for you to win in baseball any more. Isn't there anything special you'd like to accomplish next year? Something for you to aim at?"

Spahn thought for a moment. "Yes, there is something I'd like very much to accomplish," he said. "Something that's been haunting me for years. But I'm afraid it's too late now."

"Too late?" the writer asked. "Why?"

"Well, it's a sure thing Brooklyn's moving its team to Los Angeles," Warren said. Then he smiled. "Now I can never prove that I can beat the Dodgers in Ebbets Field."

WARREN SPAHN'S
BASEBALL RECORD

SPAHN, WARREN EDWARD

Born, Buffalo, New York, April 23, 1921.
Bats Left. Throws Left. Height, 6 ft. Weight, 175 pounds.

Year	Club	League	G	IP	W	L	Pct	SO	BB	H	ERA
1940	Bradford	Pony	12	66	5	4	.556	62	24	53	2.73
1941	Evansville	I.I.I.	28	212	*19	6	*.760	193	90	154	*1.83
1942	Hartford	E.L.	33	248	17	12	.586	141	130	148	1.96
1942	Boston	N.L.	4	16	0	0	.000	7	11	25	5.63
1943-44-45	Boston	N.L.			(In United States Army)						
1946	Boston	N.L.	24	126	8	5	.615	67	36	107	2.93
1947	Boston	N.L.	40	*290	21	10	.677	123	84	245	*2.33
1948	Boston	N.L.	36	257	15	12	.556	114	77	237	3.71
1949	Boston	N.L.	38	*302	*21	14	.600	*151	86	283	3.07
1950	Boston	N.L.	41	293	*21	17	.553	*191	111	248	3.16
1951	Boston	N.L.	39	311	22	14	.611	*164	*109	278	2.98
1952	Boston	N.L.	40	290	14	19	.424	*183	73	263	2.98
1953	Milwaukee	N.L.	35	266	*23	7	.767	148	70	211	*2.10
1954	Milwaukee	N.L.	39	283	21	12	.636	136	86	262	3.15
1955	Milwaukee	N.L.	39	246	17	14	.548	110	65	249	3.26
1956	Milwaukee	N.L.	39	281	20	11	.645	128	52	249	2.79
1957	Milwaukee	N.L.	39	271	*21	11	.656	111	78	241	2.69
Major League Totals			453	3232	224	146	.605	1633	938	2898	2.93

World Series Record

Year	Club	League	G	IP	W	L	Pct	SO	BB	H	ERA
1948	Boston	N.L.	3	12	1	1	.500	12	3	10	3.00
1957	Milwaukee	N.L.	2	15	1	1	.500	2	2	18	4.70
World Series Totals			5	27	2	2	.500	14	5	28	4.00

* Indicates led or tied for league lead.

Index ·

Aaron, Hank, 157, 164, 169-170, 171, 173, 178

Adcock, Joe, 129, 133, 163, 171, 178

All-Star games, 80, 85, 133, 165

American Association, 123, 125

American League teams. *See* individual listings.

Antonelli, Johnny, 83, 86, 128

Ashburn, Richie, 137-38

Baltimore Orioles, 125

Barrett, Red, 83, 93, 98-99, 110-13

Barrymore, John, 53

Basinski, Eddie, 15

Battle of the Bulge, 9-10, 65

Bauer, Hank, 171, 172, 173, 175

Bearden, Gene, 96, 99, 108

Belgium, 65

Berra, Yogi, 171, 173-174

Bickford, Vern, 82, 93, 94, 99, 128

Billy Mitchell Field, 161

Boone, Ray, 104

Boston Braves, 13, 26, 27-28, 29, 30, 44-49, 50-53, 55-60, 66-67, 68-71, 72-81, 82-95, 96-109, 110-124, 125-26, 128. *See also* Milwaukee Braves.

Boston fans, their attitude towards Braves, 56, 78, 82, 85-86, 95, 126, 128, 130, 135

Boston *Herald*, 121

Boston, Massachusetts, 71-72, 76, 82, 90, 93, 102, 125-26

Boston Red Sox, 27, 78, 95

Boudreau, Lou, 96, 97, 98, 103-04, 106

Boyer, Kenny, 157

Bradenton (Florida) spring training camp, 110-13, 115, 126, 162

Bradford (Pennsylvania) Pony League Club, 31, 32-34, 35-38, 41, 67

Braves Field, 72, 82, 85-86, 91, 95, 125-26, 136

Brookline, Massachusetts, 85

Brooklyn Dodgers, 15, 54, 57, 75, 77, 79, 81, 83, 85, 86-90, 91-93, 119, 128, 132, 133, 142-43, 147, 148-150, 155, 156, 159, 165, 169, 180

Bruton, Bill, 129, 131, 133, 135, 157, 164

Buffalo Bisons, 17

Buffalo, New York, 15, 16, 27, 34, 40, 45, 51, 55, 61, 81

Buffalo Tech High School, 24

Buhl, Bob, 128, 164, 172, 177, 178

Burdette, Lew, 128, 133, 153-54, 164, 166-68, 172, 176, 177

Busch Stadium, 155, 160

Byrne, Tommy, 175, 176

Camp Gruber, Oklahoma, 61

Carey, Andy, 171, 175

Casenovia Post American Legion team, 20

Cavaretta, Phil, 75

Chapman, Ben, 81

Chicago Cubs, 27, 72-75, 94, 119-121, 169

Christopher, Russ, 102-03

Cincinnati Reds, 27, 57, 83, 121-22, 127, 129, 144, 155, 165

Clark, Allie, 96, 98

Cleveland Indians, 95, 96-109

Coleman, Bob, 53

Coleman, Jerry, 171, 172, 173, 175

Conatser, Clint, 108

Conley, Gene, 164

Cooney, Johnny, 47, 48, 57-58, 77, 116

Cooper, Mort, 67

Cooper, Walker, 129

Costello, Ed, 121

County Stadium, 127-28, 130-31, 134, 136, 137-38, 147, 152, 161, 170, 172, 176, 178

Covington, Wes, 178

Crandall, Del, 128, 129, 137, 141, 145-46, 164, 170, 174, 178

Crone, Ray, 164, 165

Crowe, George, 119

Cy Young Memorial Award, 179

Dark, Al, 82, 85, 100, 101, 102, 108, 115, 117

Dean, Dizzy, 121

Detroit Tigers, 35

Dittmer, Art, 129

Doby, Larry, 96, 98, 108

Donovan, Willard, 53-54, 59

Dressen, Charlie, 57, 77

Ebbets Field, 75, 86, 90, 147-48, 180

Elliott, Bob, 78, 80, 83, 100, 108

Evansville (Indiana) baseball team, 53-54, 57

Feller, Bob, 96-97, 100, 102, 121, 122

Fenway Park, 78, 95

Fernandez, Nanny, 79

Ford, Whitey, 170-72
Fort Lauderdale (Florida) spring training camp, 66

Germans, 9-13, 65-66
Goodwin, Captain Francis, 11
Gordon, Joe, 96, 98, 100, 103, 107
Gordon, Sid, 117, 122, 135
Goren, Herb, 86-87
Greenberg, Joel, 126
Grim, Bob, 176
Grimm, Charley, 123, 131-32, 133, 141, 142, 143, 147-48, 151, 162
Gromek, Steve, 96, 99
Gross, Milt, 147-48
Grove, Lefty, 179

Hack, Stan, 74
Haney, Fred, 151-52, 154-55, 158, 160-61, 162, 170, 171-72, 173-74, 175, 177
Hartford (Connecticut) baseball club, 13, 58-59, 67
Hartshorne, Oklahoma, 114, 135, 152, 166, 168
Heath, Jeff, 83
Hegan, Jim, 96, 101, 104, 107-08
Hirshberg, Al, 123
Holmes, Tommy, 82, 97, 100, 102, 108, 109, 123
Hopp, Johnny, 78
Howard, Elston, 171, 173-75
Hutchinson, Freddie, 35

International League, 17

Jeffcoat, Hal, 120
Jethroe, Sam, 118, 120
Johnson, Don, 75
Johnson, Ernie, 164, 172
Jones, Nippy, 176
Judnich, Walt, 100, 104

Kazanski, Eddie, 138
Kelley, Bill, 17-18, 19
Keltner, Ken, 96, 98, 100, 104, 107
Kennedy, Bob, 98, 108-09
Kerr, Buddy, 117
Klieman, Ed, 102
Klippstein, Johnny, 119-120
Kubek, Tony, 171, 172-73, 175

Lake City Athletic Club, 16, 18, 21
Lake City A.C. Midgets, 19-20
Lanier, Max, 122
Lemon, Bob, 96, 106, 108
Lewis, Duffy, 132
Livingston, Mickey, 75
Logan, Johnny, 120, 128, 129, 131, 164, 173, 175, 176, 178
Los Angeles, California, 180
Lowrey, Peanuts, 75
Luxembourg, 65

McCormick, Frank, 83
McCormick, Mike, 83, 97, 103, 108
McDougald, Gil, 171, 173-74
Maglie, Sal, 122

Manning Vaughan Memorial Plaque, 159

Mantle, Mickey, 171, 173, 175

Mantilla, Felix, 176

Marshall, Willard, 117

Martin, Pepper, 114

Masi, Phil, 74, 75, 79-80, 81, 82, 87-89, 97, 108

Mathews, Ed, 129, 133, 136, 158, 164, 176, 178

Menzerman, Billy, 21

Merullo, Lenny, 74

Miksis, Eddie, 120

Milwaukee Baseball Writers Association, 159

Milwaukee Braves, 125-138, 139-150, 151-159, 160-180; *See also* Boston Braves.

Milwaukee Brewers, 123, 125, 129

Milwaukee fans, their attitude towards Braves, 127-28, 131, 133-36, 143, 156, 161-62, 170, 177-78

Milwaukee, Wisconsin, 125-27, 128, 134, 161, 177-78

Miracle Team, 82

Mitchell, Dale, 96, 98, 100, 102, 106

Mitchell, Jerry, 117

Moon, Wally, 158

Most Valuable Player, 80, 159, 178

Muncrief, Bob, 105

Municipal League, 16, 21

Municipal Stadium, 99, 100

Murff, Bob, 164

Musial, Stan, 157-58

Myers, Billy, 25-26, 27-28, 30, 55

National League teams. *See* individual listings.

Nazis, 9-13

New York City, 65, 71

New York Giants, 75, 83, 117, 122, 139, 142, 144, 149, 151, 164, 165, 169

New York *Post*, 117, 147-48

New York *Sun*, 86

New York Yankees, 27, 50, 83, 95, 170-177

Nicholson, Bill "Swish," 75

9th Armored Division, 65

O'Connell, Danny, 163, 165

Onslow, Jack, 32-34, 35-39, 41

Pafko, Andy, 75, 128, 129, 133, 135, 175, 178

Paige, Satchel, 96, 103

Passeau, Claude, 73, 74

Pendleton, Jim, 129, 137

Perini, Lou, 116, 117, 125-26

Perkins, Charlie, 17-18

Philadelphia Athletics, 83

Philadelphia Phillies, 81, 83, 93, 116, 132, 136, 137-38

Phillips, Taylor, 164

Pinelli, Babe, 54, 101

Pittsburgh Pirates, 15, 78, 83, 119, 144, 151, 155, 159

Pittsburgh, Pennsylvania, 70, 71, 72

Polo Grounds, 151
Potter, Nelson, 83, 87, 100-102

Queen Mary, The, 65
Quinn, John, 66, 69, 70-71, 77, 114-15

Raffensberger, Boots, 123
Ramsdell, Willard, 119
Randolph Field, 51
Reese, Pee Wee, 54, 81, 87
Reimann, Brooksie, 62, 64
Reimann, Roy, 61-63
Remagen Bridge, 9-14, 60, 65
Remagen, Germany, 11-12
Repulski, Rip, 157-58
Rhine River, 9, 65
Rickert, Marv, 97, 107, 108
Roberts, Robin, 136
Robinson, Eddie, 96, 101, 104, 107
Robinson, Jackie, 54, 87-89, 91-92
Rochester, New York, 83
Roe, Preacher, 87, 91
Rookie-of-the-Year award, 85
Russell, Jim, 83
Rust, Lieutenant Colonel Clayton A., 11
Ryan, Connie, 83, 138

Sain, Johnny, 56, 67, 78, 82, 85, 86, 91, 93, 96-97, 98-99, 100, 109, 115
St. Claire, Ebba, 120, 129
St. Louis Browns, 83, 125

St. Louis Cardinals, 66, 67, 72, 79-80, 83, 85, 91, 93, 114, 122, 128-131, 155-159, 163, 165, 168, 169
Salkeld, Bill, 83, 97, 98, 101, 102-04, 107, 108
San Antonio (Texas) spring training camp, 44, 45-49, 50-51
Sanford (Florida) spring training camp, 56-57
Sauer, Hank, 121
Schoendienst, Red, 165, 173, 176
Scotland, 65
Seattle (Washington) baseball team, 78
Serena, Bill, 119, 121
Shantz, Bobby, 172
Shoun, Clyde, 83
Sisti, Sebastian "Sibby," 28, 109, 128, 131, 135
Skowron, Bill, 171
Smalley, Roy, 120, 121
South Park High School, 21-25, 30
Southard, Lorene, 62, 64, 67-72, 76. *See also* Spahn, Mrs. Lorene.
Southworth, Billy, 66-67, 71, 72-75, 76, 85, 90-91, 94, 98, 100-101, 102, 106-07, 111-13, 115, 116, 117-18, 123
Spahn, Ed (father), 16-21, 24-25, 27-30, 31-32, 34-35, 40-45, 51, 55, 81

Spahn, Gregory Dee (son), 94, 152-54

Spahn, Mrs. (mother), 15-16

Spahn, Mrs. Lorene (wife), 76, 85, 93-94, 102, 114, 126, 152, 166-67, 168. *See also* Southard, Lorene.

Spahn, Warren Edward, is taught baseball by father, 16-19; first base his position, 19; plays for Lake City A. C. Midgets, 20; learns to pitch, 20; plays with American Legion team, 20; pitches for high school team, 23-24; is scouted by Boston Braves, 25-26; signs with them, 30; reports to Pony League club, 33; hurts left shoulder, 33-34; returns home for rest, 34; reinjures shoulder, 37; his father seriously ill, 40; gets job as baggage checker, 40; feels father's illness his fault, 42; reports for spring training, 46; pitches batting practice without pain, 46-48; wears number 13, 50; is hit in face by ball, 51; his nose is broken, 52; is given nickname, 53; is sent to Three-I League, 53; perfects first base pick-off motion, 53-54; his 1941 record, 54-55; his delivery considered flawless, 57; is to open 1942 season with Braves, 57-58; is sent down to Hartford, 58-59; reports back to Braves, 59; his 1942 record, 59; is drafted, 60; his World War II service, 9-14, 61-66; meets Lorene Southard, 64; receives Bronze Star, 65; is wounded, 13-14, 66; is commissioned second lieutenant, 66; returns home, 68; Braves still interested in, 68; postpones wedding, 70; rejoins Braves, 70; works arm back into shape, 72; is used in relief, 73-75; is knocked out of box in first starting assignment, 75; wins five straight, 76; marries Lorene, 76; loses four games in a row, two to Dodgers, 77; his 1946 record, 77; finds out he "telegraphs" his pitches, 77; eliminates flaw in delivery, 77; develops extra pitch, 77; wins first eight games in 1947, 78; is not receiving team support, 78-79, 80; unveils new slow curve, 79, 80; his 1947 record, 80; named to All-Star team, 80; is 1947 pitching sensation, 80-81; loses effectiveness, 84; wins only game at Ebbets Field, 90; picks Robinson off first base twice in one game, 92; birth of son, 94; his 1948 record, 94; Braves win National League race, 94; is knocked out of box in second series game, 98; wins fifth game in relief, 102-05; relieves in sixth game, 107-09; buys Oklahoma ranch, 114; signs 1949 contract after holding out, 114-15; wins game despite dispirited team, 116-17; his 1949 record, 117; his 1950 record, 118; continues to lead in strikeouts, 118; his 1951 record, 118; 1952 his first losing season, 118-123; sets strikeout record, 121-22; is outstanding pitcher in National League, 122-23; feels pang of regret at leaving Boston, 126; wins 1953 opener in Milwaukee, 129-131; is winning pitcher in 1953 All-Star game, 133; his 1953 record, 136; misses perfect no-hit game, 137-38; has knee operation, 140; his confidence slips, 141; his 1954 record, 142; goes through second knee operation, 142; his 1955 record, 142; realizes his fast ball is gone, 144; develops sinker pitch, 145; is unhappy about juggling of pitching rotation when playing Ebbets Field, 147-48; sinker pitch works, 149, 151; loses heartbreaker, 156-58; is honored by Milwaukee Baseball Writers, 159; wins fourth straight game on thirty-sixth birthday, 164; oil struck on his property, 166; establishes new shutout record, 169; Braves win 1957 National League pennant, 170; is knocked out of box in first series game, 172; is winning pitcher in fourth game, 172-75; named to start seventh game but is sick with flu, 177; sees Braves win 1957 World Series, 177; his 1957 record, 179; gets Cy Young Memorial Award, 179; regrets he will no longer be able to disprove his Ebbets Field "jinx," 180

Speaker, Tris, 133
Staley, Gerry, 128, 131
Stanky, Eddie, 83, 97, 103, 109, 117
Stengel, Casey, 13, 50, 55-56, 58-59, 60, 170, 172
Stewart, Bill, 97
Stuka bombers, 9-10
Surkont, Max, 128, 132

Tampa, Florida, 57
Thomson, Bobby, 164, 165
Thorpe, Bob, 129
Three-I League, 53
Tipton, Eric, 105
Torgeson, Earl, 78, 82, 91, 100, 102, 115

Torre, Frank, 173
Tucker, Thurman, 107, 108
Tulsa, Oklahoma, 62, 64, 67, 72, 76
276th Engineer Combat Battalion, 9-12, 65-66

V-2 bombs, 11
Veeck, Bill, 125
Voiselle, Bill, 83, 106-07

Waitkus, Eddie, 138
Walters, Bucky, 57
Webb, Sam, 117
Wehmeier, Herman, 156, 158
White, Ernie, 67, 69
World War II, 9-14, 56, 58, 60, 61-66

Yankee Stadium, 170-72, 177

Zoldak, Sam, 96